Perspectives in American History

No. 37

SOCIALIZATION OF THE
NEW ENGLAND CLERGY
1800 TO 1860

SOCIALIZATION
OF THE
NEW ENGLAND CLERGY
1800 TO 1860

GORDON A. RIEGLER

PORCUPINE PRESS
Philadelphia

First edition 1945
(Greenfield: The Greenfield Printing and
Publishing Co., 1945)

Reprinted 1979 by
PORCUPINE PRESS, INC.
Philadelphia, Pennsylvania 19107

Library of Congress Cataloging in Publication Data

Riegler, Gordon Arthur, 1901-
    Socialization of the New England clergy, 1800 to 1860.

    (Perspectives in American history ; no. 37)
    Reprint of the 1945 ed. published by Greenfield Print. and
Pub. Co., Greenfield, Ohio.
    Bibliography: p.
    Includes index.
    1.   New England — Church history.   2.   Clergy —
New England.   3.   Church and social problems — New
England.   I.   Title.   II.   Series: Perspectives in
American history (Philadelphia)   ;   no. 37.
BR530.R5   1979   277.4   79-13027

Manufactured in the United States of America

TO

My Aunt, Mrs. Kathryn Mayberry

TABLE OF CONTENTS

PREFACE

This is not a doctoral dissertation, nor does the author make any pretension of having written the last word on the subject to be discussed in the ensuing pages. He has read rather extensively however, made copious notes, and has tried to report faithfully what he has found, even to the extent of being repetitious at times. It is admitted that the term "New England Clergy" has been loosely employed, and that under its mantle will be found Congregationalists, Unitarians, Universalists, some Presbyterians and, perhaps, some others. As anyone who has studied this period in American church history well knows, it is not always easy or even possible to identify the denominational affiliation of all ministers accurately. This is especially true of Presbyterian and Congregational ordained religious leaders, who co-operated so closely under the Plan of Union from 1801 to 1837, and to a lesser degree to 1852. But the matter of denomination was not the most important issue in this discussion; it was not the purpose of this work to glorify any body of ministers, but rather to present some light on the proclamation of social ideals. Reason for choosing the New England Clergy was due to the fact that they left, on the whole, much more printed evidence of their views than any other group. Their position could be ascertained more readily than that of other communions.

To the New York Public Library, the Congregational and Unitarian Libraries and the Public Library of Boston, to the Cincinnati Public Library and members of their staffs who were so helpful, and to Dr. Joseph F. Fletcher, of the Graduate School of Applied Religion, of the Episcopal Theological Seminary of Cambridge, the writer wishes to express his gratitude.

GORDON A. RIEGLER

St. Stephen's Rectory
Cincinnati, Ohio
February 16, 1945

CHAPTER I

INTRODUCTION

Did the New England minister say or do anything about any of the social issues between 1800 and 1860? Casual consideration of the subject could easily persuade one that practically nothing was done in the United States, before the Civil War, to apply the ethical and moral principles inherent in Jesus' gospel to the social problems of the day. In fact an outstanding sociologist, Professor Emory S. Bogardus, tells us explicitly that for centuries the social principles of Christianity, springing from the messages of the Hebrew prophets and the teachings of Jesus, were forgotten until about 1885.[1] American church historians seem inclined to support this view. *The Story of Religions in America*, by William Warren Sweet, contains only two pages on the "social gospel," of post Civil War years, with nothing to indicate any previous interest in the matter.[2] In *The March of Faith*, Winfred E. Garrison has a chapter on the Church finding the human race.[3] Since Professor Garrison, in this volume, deals with the era dating from 1865, his chapter covers the later period. Still more recently Charles Edward Hopkins has written: *The Rise of the Social Gospel in American Protestantism, 1865-1915.* On the surface at least, this would seem to be sufficient evidence for believing that there was no attempt between 1800 and 1860, to socialize the mind of the Church — at least none worthy of mention.

A little probing, however, brings some contradictory facts to light. *Christian Hope for World Society*, by John T. McNeill, leads one to suspect that 1885 is not quite the high board fence it once was, separating two distinct eras in relation to Christian social thought and action, to the discredit of the earlier age. Upon reading Garrison's chapter,[4] the student is inclined to the view that he does not really mean what the title implies: namely that the earlier religious leaders had nothing pertinent to say about social issues. He names William Ellery Channing, Horace Bushnell and Theodore Parker as clergymen who rendered notable service, especially Bushnell, in the socialization of Christianity, though he does not happen to employ the phrase. Professor Garrison compares them favorably with Carlyle, Kingsley, Maurice and Ruskin, the English pioneer socializers. They made a beginning in the awakening of the Christian social conscience.[5] In addition to the afore-mentioned New England clergymen, Hopkins pays tribute to Joseph Tuckerman, Edward Everett Hale and Orville Dewey.[6] Another scholar, Henry Steele Commager, has a chapter dealing with the subject,[7] in which he reveals the breadth of Theodore Parker's interest, and includes therein the names of some of his well-known associates. What is perhaps even more interesting and illuminating is the fact that Father D. T. McColgan has written, and the Catholic University of America Press has published an excellent work: *Joseph Tuckerman, Pioneer in American Social Work,* which is the story of a New England clergyman, who began his Unitarian Ministry-at-Large in Boston, in 1826, and through whose influence similar work was started in Liverpool, London, Manchester and some other English cities.[8].

All this is suggestive of the fact that there may be an unexplored field of social interest on the part of the religious leadership in the years 1800 to 1860, not yet generally known, which may modify the conclusions of sociologists and historians hitherto expressed in their writings.

So far we have only hinted that something of a social consciousness existed among some of the outstanding New England clergy, and therefore among the lesser clergy too, for it is not too much to say that the distinguished preachers of the early nineteenth century greatly influenced their less famous brethren in the ministry. But the student of sociology and history wants something more tangible than mere hints. Is there anything definite, then, to indicate an awareness on the part of churchmen of the existence of social problems, and that the Church had a part to play in their solution? This is a fair question, for the answer to which we must examine the messages of the New England ministers.[9] By fitting together their various statements, as one would gather and put into place the many pieces of a picture-puzzle, the student is able to compile the story of their social interest.

Dr. Horace Bushnell told his Hartford congregation that the Church should be more interested in social problems. *Preaching on Sermons for the New Life,* one Sunday he chose to deal with "Respectable Sin," in which he informed his hearers that there was not enough realism in religion. The gamblers, drunkards, thieves, prostitutes and the victims of these evils were not in the pew in any number.[10] A hint of his social philosophy may be seen in the following: " . . . existence itself can be only worthless, save as we lay hold of each other in some fellow feeling, and fulfill answering conditions of social benefit."[11] He preached on "God Organizing in the Church His Eternal Society," in which he emphasized the need for a socialized Christianity: "God help us all to have our future in it, by the law of social right, in that universal ownership conferred on each by the everlasting society of all."[12]

The Rev. J. I. T. Coolidge, who delivered the dedicatory sermon of the Thirteenth (Unitarian) Congregational Church, Boston, May 3, 1848, was also quite explicit. Maybe the pioneer characteristically feels that he is more alone than he actually is, and so there is a bit of pathos in his statement that: "Long was it before any voice was lifted in opposition to any existing order of society."[13] But he had hopes. Christianity was always at work to prepare men for a better world, not in some vague hereafter, but in this life. Humanity had now reached the point, where Christianity was being applied to social issues, and it was pleading for human rights as never before. It was investigating evils afflicting mankind with a thoroughness hitherto unknown.[14]

Not everyone agreed with Bushnell and Coolidge. It would have been too much to expect it, for, as we shall see, there were those who profited by the world as it was. Unfortunately there is usually at least one clergyman who is out-of-sympathy with social preaching. So the Rev. Samuel Barrett, who spoke on Fast Day before the Twelfth Congregational Church in Boston, April 10, 1851, complained of too much being said. Strange theories were advocated, which among other things would disturb business, upset the social order, and work some harm to religion — perhaps the loss of wealthy contributors(?). If these views were carried to their logical conclusions, men (undoubtedly those who were enriched by the status-quo) had every right to fear for the future.[15] Yet it would be as untrue as it would be unkind to convey the impression that Barrett, a Unitarian, was hardhearted toward the underprivileged masses. He was one of the leaders in support of Tuckerman's work in Boston.[16]

Defenders of social preaching arose, while some others apparently wished to *straddle* the issue, or held that reforms of a social nature should be left to societies organized for that specific purpose.[17] In 1856, Madison, Wisconsin, although incorporated as a city in that year, was still a frontier settlement, yet not so remote that the Congregational minister, the Rev. Nathaniel H. Eggleston, of that place, refrained from rebuking those who looked askance at Christianity interested in social problems. He knew there were good people "whose religion is of such a narrow type" that they were "fearfully shocked" whenever it was "brought into contact with the everyday affairs of life."[18] So long as the preacher contented himself with attacks on evil in the abstract, so long as his exhortations were very general, nothing was said in opposition to him; but let a man apply Christian principles to specific wrongs, then the uproar began.[19]

These preachers knew their rights and duties, and had some ideas of the kind of world in which they wanted to live. They did not propose to be intimidated or to be bribed. As early as 1815, Daniel Dana, later to become president of Dartmouth College for a time, was aware of Christian responsibilities. The Christian man was "a friend to the poor, a patron to the oppressed, a benefactor to society, a blessing to his species,"[20] and persons who lacked a sense of social obligation simply were not Christians.[21]

Caleb Stetson, the Unitarian minister at Medford, about 1846, did not agree that social issues should be kept out of the pulpit, [22] and there were others sympathetic to his view. There was Jacob Abbott, Congregational clergyman, educator and author, who wanted to live in a world where right human relationships prevailed, where commerce between people was based on the fundamentals of character.[23] Although given somewhat to moralizing, this did not prevent him from attempting to create wholesome social attitudes.[24] William T. Dwight, J. S. Davies, T. B. Thayer, Frederick H. Hedge, and William Ellery Channing, to mention some of them, were among those who agreed with Stetson. Hedge, a pastor in Bangor, was confident that one did not need to be a communist or a socialist in order to believe that Christianity gave new meaning to the word *society*. When Jesus said, "All ye are brethren," he spoke that word which meant a new era. [25] Thayer, a New England Universalist, declined to accept any notion of religion, which limited it to "prayers

and hymns and sermons."[26] It had to do with the whole of
life, and Dwight, of the Third Congregational Church, Portland, Maine, agreed with him defining the broad boundaries
within which the Christian minister was at home. "Man individually, man in his domestic, social and civil relations,
man as the ruled and the ruler, man as combined into parties
of every name or as constituting communities and nations,
are all included."[27] It does not require much imagination to
see where that led. Man as a person has need for food,
clothing, shelter, companionship, culture, learning, religion.
Both as an individual and as a member of a family, his concern was with health, housing, etc. Relations with others
and citizenship were involved, even international affairs. Of
course Dwight did not mention these — may not have been
aware of them as problems of a social nature — but his defense of the minister's broad field in which to operate
would one day bring the clergyman to them all. He had
sharp words for any who would limit the preacher's domain.
Such a man he called a "lawless invader."[28]

Did someone accuse the New England clergy in failing
to preach the gospel? Discussion of social questions in the
pulpit in our own generation has so often called forth this ac-
cusation that it needs no citation. At any rate, Davies, of
Concord, held that the preachers tried to apply Biblical and
Christian principles in order to promote "education, justice,
and humanity."[29] The well-being of society was their goal.[30]
He knew the objections, and he had his answer. The pulpit
must be free; no minister was to be bribed or intimidated, or
silenced; if he were, then that man was no longer an "ambas-
sador of Christ."[31]

An ordination service was a good time, at least Channing seemed to think so, to say some things on the subject. Other ministers and the young candidate were there to
be influenced. If they reacted favorably, more than likely

they would take it up too. A representative congregation of lay people also came to ordinations; it was opportune to let them know something of the minister's relation to society and to social questions. So Dr. Channing, who was asked to deliver the sermon, at the ordination of his new assistant at Federal St. Church, Boston, challenged Christians to look about them, and then say if they could that they lived in the best possible world. A man who was not burdened by what he saw in society was not fit for holy orders. This eminent divine was persuaded that a consecrated ministry could and should do something to bring about a better social order.[32] But ordinations did not provide the only opportunity for emphasizing the social aspects of Christianity. Although such service clubs as Kiwanians, Rotarians and Lions are twentieth century affairs for business and professional men, where luncheon speakers are heard, nevertheless the early nineteenth century was not entirely without their counterpart. At any rate the pulpit notables of that day did more than deliver sermons to congregations. Channing was invited to address a group of business men in Philadelphia, where he spoke on "The Present Age."[33] Always the gentleman, Channing was glad to come to them, to serve them, but to be most useful, his lecture must "be frank, honest, free."[34] "He who speaks must speak what he thinks, — speak courteously, but uncompromisingly."[35] He thought that much speech-making in America was unprofitable, because of the fear of offending either the majority or "the fashionable or refined."[36] It was a polite man's well-mannered way of warning his hearers that he had come to tell them the things which he believed, with which they, no doubt, would disagree, and not, perhaps, the things they thought they wanted to hear.

He came from Boston to tell them that the privileged classes were diminishing, while the whole of humanity was assuming a new importance: "The multitude is rising from the dust."[37] Many of the differences between men were on the surface only — rank was a matter of disguise, underneath there was a common humanity. Every individual had powers worthy of development. The importance "of man as man" was spreading "silently but surely."[38] He knew what many of the favored few were saying. They accused this age of being "wild, lawless, presumptuous, without reverence."[39] Men were being selfish in wanting to leave their ranks; masses were forsaking their natural leaders; the poor were being pitted against the rich; a dangerous fanaticism was abroad, and that continuance in this way only brewed future social storms.[40]

"Christianity," he said, "is a pledge of a social order which none of us sufficiently prize."[41] It would come, and he did not believe there was valid reason for fearing it, even though the prosperous were afraid. It would not hurt society to uplift the masses. He knew his history, and from history he read that: "Communities fall by the vices of the great, not the small."[42]

Modern medical science might not agree with the Rev. Wm. R. Alger, the Congregational minister at Roxbury, that the cholera epidemic of his day was the result of "neglected and accumulated evils, from the mass of physical, social, and personal sins."[43] But it is hard to see how the social engineer, the humanitarian, and the preacher of the social gospel could disagree with his premise that gigantic and hideous social ills afflicted mankind; that God, a loving Father, provided the means for social well-being, and that he did require Christian men to produce a better world.[44]

It would seem, perhaps, that Alger's social consciousness arose out of the plague. On the other hand, it may have been that he regarded the pestilence as an admirable occasion on which to give vent to thoughts and feelings he long cher-

ished. We do know this, the War, with Mexico, protested as
we shall see later, by many clergymen, brought forth social
utterances, such as that made by C. A. Bartol, of West
Church, Boston: "The disorders and wrongs and sufferings
of human life demand rectification. . . ."[45] Preaching on
The Prevalent Sins of the Times, the Rev. C. M. Nickels,
of the Evangelical Congregational Church, Gloucester, denounced slavery, and he discovered that man had certain
rights, which were being violated, and that was sin."[46]

Evidence that men were for or against social progress,
for or against the Church lifting its voice in behalf of such
progress is seen in the foregoing pages. But in every movement there are also some middle-of-the-road men; men who
bridge the gap between those who take one side or the other.
They may compromise on some low level, or they may be
moved by high considerations to bring factions together, to
interpret one side to the other, and to make way for adjust-
ments. Of the latter order seems to be the Rev. Joseph Eldridge, pastor of the Congregational Church, Norfolk, Connecticut, who spoke on *Reform and Reformers,* a sermon delivered in November, 1843. He was convinced that God used
human agencies to reform mankind.[47] But that reform in
society will come gradually and without "any radical change
in the characters of its constituent members."[48] Reformers
should be men of wisdom and discretion, not destructive, but
objective. Ancient evils will not be done away in a day, so
we must do what we can and patiently await the results.[49]

Social consciousness was developing among the clergy.
Ordinarily, we think of Lyman Beecher, of Boston and Cincinnati, as the defender of orthodox theology; yet he did
not wish social ills to flourish any more than he wanted
heresy to thrive. He expected religion to do something.
Civil laws by themselves could not "prevent social evils that
annoy, or coerce virtues that enrich society. . . ."[50] While

the Rev. Richard R. Elliot, minister at Watertown, Massachusetts, as early as 1816, held to the opinion that true religion produces right social attitudes, such as understanding, justice, sharing and integrity.[51]

The Rev. Orville Dewey, minister of the Unitarian Church of the Messiah, in New York City, was keenly aware of the social issues, and he delivered a whole series of sermons incorporated in a two-volume work: *Moral Views of Commerce, Society, and Politics.* He saw the social question forcing its way into the pulpit with the opening of the War of 1812. Dewey held that religion was to be defined broadly, so as to deal with all the activities and thoughts of men,[52] and in connection with social evils, he hurled the question at his generation: "Do we live in an age where the antiquity of a[n] evil is held to be good argument for its perpetuity?"[53] In 1834, Calvin Lincoln, minister of the Congregational Church at Fitchburg, Massachusetts, knew that "men must understand the nature of their social relations."[54] The common good must be placed above private gain. Principles of a social nature must have their way to penetrate and modify society.[55]

So something of a social philosophy was being developed; social action was becoming a fact. Not every clergyman who uttered a social principle saw it applied in all directions, as we shall see. Nevertheless voices were raised in behalf of better education, better health, better housing. Duelling, liquor, gambling, rights of women and children, immigration, agriculture, race relations, working conditions, wages, better government, war and peace all came in for some discussion — more or less. The ensuing chapters will relate the story of efforts to socialize the Church and Society on specific issues. Thus it was that William Furness, Unitarian minister in Philadelphia, could speak of "the great social law of Christianity."[56]

CHAPTER II

EDUCATION

It was no accident that the New England minister of the early nineteenth century was interested in education. Professor Jernegan tells us that no colonial enterprise ever embraced so many college men as did that of Massachusetts Bay.[1] Pilgrims, too, were influenced by their beloved and educated pastor, John Robinson, who served them from about 1608 to 1625, though prevented from coming to America and separated from his American flock till his death in 1625.[2] So the Dame Schools were set up in Plymouth Colony at a very early date,[3] and Harvard, the college in the wilderness, was established in 1636.[4] Six colleges and universities: Bowdoin, Dartmouth, Harvard, Marietta, Williams and Yale, are listed in the *Congregational Year Book for* 1940, as being founded by them before the nineteenth century.[5] Academies. supplying the needs of high schools in those days, were also founded, among them both Phillips, Andover, Massachusetts, and Phillips, Exter, New Hampshire.[6] Thus it was natural that the clergy who figured so largely in the founding of earlier institutions of learning,[7] should continue this work into the nineteenth century.

The Office and Influence of Evangelical Pastors was the title of a sermon delivered by the Rev. Nathaniel Bouton, pastor of the First Congregational Church, Concord, New Hampshire. at the installation of the Rev. John Smith. pastor of First Church, Exeter, in 1829. In this message, he took the stand that: "The influence of Pastors on the intellectual character of society is visible in the fact, that they are the patrons of education in all its branches."[8] Bouton saw them diffuse knowledge by writing and preaching, and

11

he knew they sought out and encouraged promising young people to extend their education.[9]

When Dr. Leonard Bacon, minister of Center Church, New Haven, and later a Yale professor, addressed the Phi Beta Kappa Society at Dartmouth, he pointed out the value of the educated man to the community. Such a man was a neighbor, who by influence and not by force, elevated the reading habits of the people, promoted libraries, improved the schools, and taught the people a higher standard of living. Incidentally Bacon did not like the way foreign literature was being read in the United States; it tended, he thought, to make the American rich believe they were better than their less fortunate fellows, and to make the poor feel oppressed.[10]

Armed with statistics, Theodore Parker, the Unitarian pastor at West Roxbury, later famous preacher at Melodeon Hall, Boston, where he was an outcast among the clergy of his day, but owner of the largest private library in America,[11] called attention to the ignorance in Boston. He knew there were 4,948 children of school age, i. e., four to fifteen, who were not in school, of whom at least 2,000 were turned into the streets as young vagrants. What was to happen to them? Given the right opportunity, they might become good citizens. Otherwise a large percentage of them would surely follow the pursuits of crime.[12] In such a situation, Parker called on the Christian Church to "lead the movement for the public education of the people."[13] It became the duty of the State to provide free common schools, free high schools instead of academies (where tuition was paid), and free colleges rather than tuition-supported and endowed private institutions, he declared in his address on "The Public Education of the People," delivered in 1849.[14] Especially was he concerned with the education of the laboring classes,[15] and he placed high responsibility on the American scholar.[16]

Others disagreed with Parker's views on theology, but many of them did see eye to eye with him on the necessity of education. Francis Convers, the Congregational minister at Watertown, knew democratic forms of government depended on it in order to survive. "It is impossible that an ignorant people can long value or wield the power of self-government."[17]

William Seaver, evidently a resident of Washington, D. C., or a visitor to that city, was murdered on or about July 6, 1821. So the Rev. Robert Little, Unitarian minister in that place, made it the occasion for speaking on: *Ignorance, the Parent of Crime,* in which he held that great crimes were usually the result of ignorance.[18] If they lacked education in earlier years; if they failed in later years to add to what they had previously learned, men tended to turn to crime.[19]

Hope for the future lay in superior education, thought another Unitarian, the Rev. Lemuel Capen, of Massachusetts.[20] Still other Unitarians and Trinitarians were in agreement. Among the former were J. S. Buckminster, brilliant Boston cleric, Samuel J. May, minister of the Church of the Messiah, in Syracuse, Abiel Abbott, the stormy petrel of Connecticut, and Channing. In the latter group were: Timothy Dwight, the president of Yale, Jacob Abbott, the children's story-teller, Charles G. Finney, president of Oberlin and evangelist, and Horace Bushnell.

Finney, who was a trained lawyer, a successful evangelist, pastor of Broadway Tabernacle, New York City, and second president of Oberlin, to mention only a few of his attainments, concluded that the best inheritance a father could leave his son was not wealth, but education for life.[21] The Rev. N. H. Chamberlain, a Massachusetts man, whose denominational relations are a little uncertain, expressed the acme of faith in education. It was the duty of the State to aid the individual in the attainment of the highest intellectual achievement through a regularly established system of education.[22] Did someone question the wisdom of democracy in higher education? He had his reply ready. Universal university training would bring us "centuries nearer the attainment of perfect liberty."[23] But who would perform the services of manual labor if everyone had an A. B. degree, or its equivalent? That evidently worried those who were unaccustomed to it. So great was his confidence in the maximum of learning for all that he answered: "then the wood would hew and the water draw itself,"[24] a prediction less farfetched in 1945 than some eighty years ago, when he made it!

Dr. Joseph Tuckerman, Unitarian minister-at-large, was keenly interested in education. He became associated with Moses Grant, in 1827, on the Boston Primary School Committee, and was chosen to represent District 5, which he did whole-heartedly. At his request a sub-committee was selected to find out what children were being excluded from the city's schools — he was made the chairman, and so effective was his work that in the following year ten new schools were opened for children above the age of seven, but not yet ready for Grammar School.[25]

Defenders and improvers of the public schools were Samuel May and Horace Bushnell. May took a prominent part in effecting an organization at Hartford, Connecticut, when he lived there, the purpose of which was to improve public education in the state by improving the public schools. His efforts were put forth in 1827.[26] Bushnell thought he saw a threat to the public school system in the attitude of the Roman Catholic Church, with its parochial schools. So, in Hartford, on March 25, 1853, he delivered his address: "Common Schools,"[27] in which he said: "Here we take our stand, and upon this we may insist as being a great American institution. . . . one that is inseparably joined to the fortunes of the republic. . . ."[28] Our common schools brought together the rich and poor, while in the select schools of the rich, the pupils learned to despise the poor, and the excluded poor on the outside hated the rich. Public schools were a protection against factions, [29] and must not be given up for any reason. [30]

Timothy Dwight, president of Yale, and a man whose social vision has been questioned, did think higher education should be extended, and augmented by public libraries.[31] To the libraries and schools, the pastor of Northborough Church, Massachusetts, the Rev. Joseph Allen, advocated the addition of lectureships or lyceums.[32]

But it was more than superstitious faith! *Education* was not some magic word, blindly trusted. Both Jacob Abbott, the story-telling educator, who was trained at Andover and ordained to the Gospel Ministry in the Congregational fellowship, and Francis Convers were dissatisfied with the existing system, as was also Channing. Abbott knew the inadequacies. It was his opinion that "the atmosphere of the school-room withers and blights, as often as it protects and sustains."[33] He definitely advocated a psychological approach to the teaching of pupils. Study them individually and meet their needs as individuals! Above all the teacher was not to regard his own task as dull routine, but something vastly more important.[34] Convers, too, knew the errors. Too often the child's mind was looked upon as a kind of empty receptacle, only waiting to be filled. But minds possessed dormant qualities to be awakened and stimulated; faculties which needed certain materials for development. The real purpose of education was to discipline and strengthen, rather than to fill the mind. In this process of teaching, the importance of indirect influence must not be overlooked.[35]

Dr. Channing did not think much of education which was content to crowd the mind with so much knowledge, teach the mechanics of reading, writing, spelling and arithmetic, or to tax the memory. Reading was only an instrument — education should teach a boy how best to use the tool. Youth should be taught to observe the relation between cause and effect, the connection between events, to discern general principles. "A spirit of humanity should be breathed into him from all his studies."[36] Buildings, equipment and courses of study were important, but the kind of education he advocated needed something more important even than these. Education that was to benefit all, regardless of economic status, and for which the entire universe was responsible, needed more great teachers.[37] True, some young folks became self-educated, so to speak. But that was no argument against schools, and equipment, and teachers. Any number of persons who were willing to squander thousands of dollars "on dress, furniture, amusements think it hard to pay comparatively small sums to the instructor".[38] Penny-pinching, when it came to education, was bad economy; it robbed children of something extremely precious, a treasure, for the loss of which there was no other compensation.[39] "Money should never be weighed against the soul of a child."[40] So, if you would improve teaching, you must have the best teachers, and to have them, you must pay an adequate stipend. "No profession should receive so liberal remuneration."[41] The advocate of education for all, the pleader for better teachers was willing to have them receive higher pay for their services than the members of his own beloved profession. How different his views from those of a modern society, which pays its corporation presidents, its motion picture stars, and its prize fighters fabulous sums; and provides even greater compensation to its unskilled workers in war industries than to its pedagogues!

He had another arrow in his quiver to shoot at vulnerable parents. What were they doing, that they did not know more about the teachers into whose hands they entrusted their children's training of mind and character? Surely they were lacking in the knowledge of those who taught their off-spring. Some of them had never even seen these instructors, and had never attempted to enquire as to the progress their children were or were not making.[42] A teacher was more important than a statesman.[43] Because of false notions concerning education, too many persons thought anybody could teach. Nothing could be more erroneous! Since the true function of education was not to fill the mind, but to develop the personality and to unfold and strengthen natural abilities, the office of instructor called for peculiar gifts.[44]

Constructive proposals were made for enlarged and improved services, including a broader curriculum. In some cases recommendations were for specific communities, and in others for the improvement of educational systems and methods universally. In the former category is the work of the Rev. Paul Dean, Boston Universalist, who in 1819 served on a special investigating committee of the local Board of Education. To this committee was assigned the task of learning which of the children, in the city, were deprived of an education for economic reasons. He signed a report which called attention to privileges which were or should be afforded to those who lived in America, and demanded as a right for underprivileged children all the advantages of an education necessary to know and to appreciate those privileges. Schools for them could be opened at public expense for a trifling amount. The result was the establishment of "Intermediate" schools.[45] Ezra S. Gannett, Channing's assistant in Federal Street Church of Christ, was convinced that among other things, this question of woman's education had been most arrogantly and improperly answered (by men).[46] Others shared with him in this view. Lemuel Capen thought that heretofore woman's education had been more ornamental than solid, and that women needed systematic and broader training.[47] Samuel J. May aired his opinions on the subject in his address on *The Revival of Education,* before the Normal Association, at Bridgewater, Massachusetts, August 8th, 1855.

Both Bushnell and Channing believed that schools should consider the needs of the farmers. Text-books on agriculture should be put into the schools, said Bushnell.[48] While Channing felt that every prospective farmer should be taught chemistry, in order that he might know the nature of the soil, the best methods of fertilizing it, etc.[49] Channing went even further in advocating an enlarged curriculum. Of the leading advanced schools in technology: Massachusetts Institute of Technology, Carnegie, Armour and California, the first is the oldest, having been founded in 1861. The Polytechnic Institute of Brooklyn was opened in 1854.[50] But fourteen years earlier (1840), Channing urged schools for the training of mechanics, who would understand machines and the laws of physics, and other practical aspects of science.[51]

But the New England clergy were not content to give vocal support only to the cause of education, or merely to serve on special school board committees. Mere talk was not enough. They had to do something about it! The American Education Society was one of the numerous organizations founded in the early half of the nineteenth century.[52] True enough, its purpose was to secure the better training of young men for the orthodox Congregational ministry,[53] *but it was an education society nevertheless.* It could not promote the cause among prospective preachers without having a few drops of knowledge, or the incentive to learn, spill among the ranks of the laity, and from 1820 to 1824, a single branch of the institution contributed $4,500.00,[54] perhaps the equivalent of $22,500.00 in modern terms.

Frequently the missionary on the frontier was the one

and only educated person in the entire community; children needed instruction and the clergyman might even need a little extra money, for his pay was pathetically small and worse, often uncertain. Consequently practical situations made the ministers educators as well.[55] But it would be grossly unfair to imply that religious leaders became teachers, wholly or even largely motivated by self-interest. In many instances it would be difficult to find any such motive. For example, when the Rev. Edward D. Griffin, of Massachusetts, was invited to preach in a certain church, he was given an honorarium of one hundred dollars. Instead of keeping it for himself, or giving it to his wife and family, he immediately turned it over to a college, probably Williams, in which he was interested.[56] Not many years after the founding of Oberlin College, that school reached a grave financial crisis. Would it be able to weather the storm, or would it be obligated, as many other schools have done, to suspend operations? The generosity of the Congregational Church, Green Bay, Wisconsin, still regarded as a wilderness by people in the East, furnished the sum of five thousand dollars, which rescued the young institution from the necessity of closing its doors.[57]

Fourteen institutions of higher learning, now extant, were founded between 1800 and 1859, which owe their origin to the Congregationalists, in some instances with the aid of the Presbyterians under the famous Plan of Union of 1801.[58] The oldest of these is Middlebury College, in Vermont, established in 1800. The Unitarian schism in New England resulted in the loss of Harvard to the Unitarians, so, in 1821, the Trinitarians founded Amherst, at Northampton.[59]

Two factors were involved in the establishment of Oberlin about 1833. A Christian colony was conceived by the Rev. John J. Shipherd and founded at Oberlin, in Ohio, which was to have its own college. Charles G. Finney tells us that about this time "the breaking up of Lane Seminary took place, on account of the prohibition by the trustees, of the discussion of slavery among the students."[60] Arthur Tappan wanted him to go to Ohio, to care for the training of those who withdrew from Lane, but he had come to no decision, as yet, when Shipherd and Asa Mahan, who had been a trustee of Lane, came to New York, offering him the chair in theology at Oberlin, which he now accepted.[61] Of the 44 students who enrolled the first term, 15 were women, this being the first college in the world to place women on an equal footing with men. Negro students, too, were made welcome. Such liberality appealed to 30 Lane students, who now moved to Oberlin, where they began the study of theology under Finney.[62]

Young graduates of Yale, Andover and other eastern institutions went West as home missionaries. They were organized into voluntary *bands*. As to Ohio, so they went to Illinois, Michigan, Wisconsin, Iowa and farther west. In 1827, under the elms in New Haven, seven students met and pledged themselves to the ministry and to education. This was the beginning of the famous Yale Band. Theron Baldwin, Julian M. Sturtevant and Edward Beecher were among the pioneers who started Jacksonville's Illinois College (1829). In 1837, Knox was founded at Galesburg. Olivet, in Michigan, was organized in 1844. Two schools: Beloit (1846) and Ripon (1851) were opened in Wisconsin. Asa Turner was in Iowa in 1843, and soon he had his Iowa Band of preachers, who were instrumental in starting Iowa College (1847), which later moved to another part of the State and became Grinnell. It seems incredible that the missionary preachers reached the Pacific Coast so early, and laid the foundations for Pacific University in Oregon (1849) and Whitman College, Washington (1859).[63]

All of these institutions, with the exception of Amherst,

for men only, were co-educational. But to meet the needs of women in a new age, the Congregational clergy played an important, if not the stellar role in the beginnings of Milwaukee-Downer (1851) and Rockford (1847), and, no doubt, had considerable to do with founding of Mt. Holyoke, all of which were women's colleges.[64]

New schools for theological education were also opened. Mention has already been made concerning Oberlin. Amherst was not the only school to be born of the Unitarian schism. Andover Theological Seminary, in the interests of orthodoxy, was organized in 1808.[65] Bangor Theological Seminary began at Hampden, Maine, in 1816, later removing to Bangor. After more than 100 years, in 1822 Yale Divinity School became a distinct division in Yale College, with Nathaniel Taylor as administrator.[66] Hartford Theological Seminary was founded in 1833, and Chicago Theological Seminary in 1855.[67]

Other institutions, too, owed much to the New England clergy, especially to the Trinitarian Congregationalists, who were very missionary-minded. Horace Bushnell played a prominent part in the founding of University of California, the largest state university in America, of which he was invited to become the first president, but declined.[68] Lake Erie College (1847), at Painesville, Ohio, a school for women; Western Reserve University (1826); Berea College, Kentucky, which opened in 1855; Union Theological Seminary, New York, as well as Auburn, now affiliated with Union, all were indebted to Congregational leadership to some extent at least. It is more than likely, too, that such leading state universities as Michigan, Minnesota and Wisonsin, all founded within the era of our interest, were in some degree responsible to the influence and efforts of some of the New England ministers for their existence.[69].

It may be that a large and influential number of the

New England clergy would have agreed with Orville Dewey's advanced idea of education, that it "in the largest sense, is the preparation of the mind for the scene in which it is set to act,"[70] for both by their words and deeds, they showed forth their feeling that it was necessary to launch a program of school-building across the nation. In promoting education for the many, in this respect at least, they were the socializers of Christianity. Theirs was heroic vision accompanied by a large scale and sacrificial service.

CHAPTER III

GAMBLING, DUELLING AND DRINKING

No amount of romanticism regarding frontier-life and the good old days can obscure the moral degeneracy of the early 1800s. It was, of course, no sudden debauch, but had been developing for a long time, as has been shown.[1] Much of the advertising of the late eighteenth and early nineteenth centuries provides a key to the low tastes of the public. Somewhat startling, but not untypical, is an advertisement appearing in the *Boston Gazette,* on October 3, 1774: "A Wet Nurse with a Young Breat of Milk wants a place in a Gentleman's Family."

Gambling was sanctioned by the best elements in society. Didn't Harvard College use the lottery to keep its doors open? No secret was made of it, for both on February 21, 1774, and again on May 5th, *Boston Gazette* contained two announcements of financing the College, five thousand dollars was the highest prize to be offered. Harvard was not alone. Dartmouth and William and Mary also employed this means of meeting obligations, and Thomas Jefferson, patron saint of democracy, tried to recoup his fortunes and save his beloved Monticello by it.[2]

As for duelling, doesn't everybody know that Lord Byron killed Mr. Chaworth in 1765, William Pitt and George Tierny, in 1796, fought each other over in England? In the Revolutionary period, in our own land, John Laurens and Charles Lee, John Cadwalader and Thomas Conway, Lachlan McIntosh and Button Gwinnett, all engaged in duels.[3] If there were fewer combats on this side of the Atlantic than on the other, it was not because Americans lacked misguided courage, but rather because we had fewer *gentlemen* to engage in the manly art. So this practice was carried over into the new century. Among those whose names are well known in American history, who took part in these contests in the 1800s, were Alexander Hamilton, Aaron Burr, Henry Clay, DeWitt Clinton, Stephen Decatur, Andrew Jackson and John Randolph.[4] Duelling in America, in the nineteenth century, we are told, was rife.[5]

The use of alcoholic beverages, too, had become a grave problem. Almost everyone was addicted to the habit. The universality of drinking is described by Prof W. W. Sweet.[6] Ordination and installation councils were not always large. In fact the delegates were frequently entertained in a single house. Records of the First Congregational Church of Ulster, in Saugerties, New York, indicate that ministers and lay delegates from but three outside congregations attended the council called to recognize the organization of that body in 1853. Yet the amount of liquor consumed was often astounding. In Revolutionary times, more than six hundred dollars was spent for entertainment of the council which met to ordain the Rev. Mr. Kilbourn of Chesterfield,[7] and we are told that as late as 1825, at the installation of Leonard Bacon, at Center Church, New Haven, drinks were provided free to all who wished them, the church generously paying the bills.[8]

So the socializers of Christianity in the early 1800s were confronted by the problems of gambling, duelling and drinking. Whether they would recognize these as social ills to be assailed and dealt with is to be shown in the succeeding pages. We shall see if the Rev. J. T. I. Coolidge was right, as applied to these evils, when he said that Christianity "is searching everywhere, and it meets no abuse, no iniquity, that it will not ere long wholly rend away and extirpate."[9]

Historically the Church has taken its stand against gambling. It was forbidden to the clergy by various Church Councils; ministers have denounced it; and Tertullian denied that any dice--player was a Christian. Yet we have seen how church institutions profited by some phase of it (p. 23). Not only lottery, but horse racing, cock fights, cards and other activities were connected with the practice. Professional gamblers travelled on the river boats of the Mississippi system,[11] on which clergymen to and from the frontier also took passage.[12] So the religious leaders had ample opportunity to become acquainted with the custom as their own observers. The Rev. Aratus Kent, a missionary to Galena, Illinois, under the auspices of the American Home Missionary Society, one of those who journeyed at least part of the way by boat, described the " 'practice of gambling' " as being " 'beyond anything I ever saw.' "[13] Kent's experience was not unusual as the unpublished correspondence of the American Home Missionary Society, housed at the Chicago Theological Seminary, shows. Both I. G. Likens, a missionary at Jacksonville, Illinois, in 1835, and S. J. Bradstreet, missionary in Cleveland, Ohio, in 1826, complained of it. Likens protested that he was obliged to conduct religious services within the sound of the gambler's voices, while they were playing their game.[14]

Gambling was frequently assailed, as indicated in the American Home Missionary Society collection. Whether Charles G. Finney included the elimination of it when he spoke of a community, as a result of his revivals, being "morally renovated,"[15] we are not certain. But the high standards maintained by Oberlin College for more than one hundred years are well known; and Finney's life and influence were interwoven with the early history of the College. It would seem, therefore, that his converts, among whom some must have been addicted to the evil, would thereafter shun it. This was an age of great theologians. Included among their number, as well as Finney, were Timothy Dwight, Leonard Woods, Edwards A. Park, Henry Ware, Lyman Beechler, Nathaniel Taylor and Nathaniel Emmons, to mention a few.[16] Perhaps they depended in large measure upon producing a right relationship with God to bring about some of the social reforms, if not all of them, and, in this expectation, they were not entirely wrong. Strong doctrine preached by revivalists produced results in the social order.[17] At any rate, we fail to find any condoning of gambling, and some churches did discipline their members for indulgence.[18] Dr. Henry Bellows, the colorful New York clergyman, did not believe you could class gambling among the amusements.[19] John Emery Abbot, Unitarian minister at Salem, Massachusetts, was very much distressed and strenuously opposed it.[20] While the fiery Lyman Beecher unhesitatingly believed that politicians guilty of this evil should be disciplined. The measure proposed was severe punishment — they should be disqualified for public office,[21] Horace Bushnell, too, went after this vice in earnest:

> Gamblers, stock speculators, panderers to vice, brokers at the ballot box in the sale of public offices, all these and such like it [the truly Christian community] will finally remove, and the sorry cant of their profession, that 'society owes them a living,' will be heard no more.[22]

No doubt lesser luminaries among the New England ministers likewise took their stand against gambling. Of course it was not always attacked by that name. Channing speaks of fighting on the exchange,[23] undoubtedly having in mind speculation in business. Not only did sermons and letters denounce it, but religious periodicals, edited by clergymen, had their say on the subject. *The Christian Journal,* for

August 21, 1829, moralised against it, under the caption: "A Singular Fact." *The Quarterly Christian Spectator* asserted that we have laws "against gambling tables in the market-places,"[24] and yet New York City had "secret gambling houses" and "a hundred and fifty or two hundred lottery offices".[25] This writer accused the patron of such places as being a public enemy.[26] While others spoke their minds against gambling, Bradstreet, of Cleveland, put his faith in some kind of organization to combat it, so he was instrumental in forming his "Moral Society," which was to attack this and other vices in an effective manner.[27] Then, there was Joseph Tuckerman, in Boston. His work as minister-at-large, to the poor and needy, threw him into many contacts with the less privileged children — those who slept in dark rooms and played in alleys; he learned about them and their habits. As a result of his observations he made some interesting classifications of them. Among the more vicious boys there were many gamblers.[28] But he had his ways of dealing with this and other evils, of which the young were victims, as we shall see in his program for and treatment of them, in the next chapter.

Historically the Church as such had been troubled by the duel, and issued edicts against it.[29] Did Horace Bushnell oppose it? Perhaps so! "In a really Christian community," he said, "no man goes abroad having his bosom lined with deadly weapons."[30] Forthright in their denunciation of it were both the Rev. Charles Hoover, of Newark, New Jersey, and William W. Patton. So also did M. A. H. Niles and Lyman Beecher take their stand against it.

Hoover thought it was doubly diabolical, since (1) it involved deliberate murder, and (2) suicide. The Press, the Political Leadership, the Home and the Church, all were duty-bound to mould public opinion against it and to denounce it.[31] Patton agreed that to kill one in a duel was murder, and to vote for any man guilty of fighting a duel was a crime.[32] No doubt Patton had in mind Henry Clay, who that year was a candidate for the United States presidency.[33] Niles thought it absurd to believe that aiming a pistol and firing at another could possibly determine who was right and who was wrong much less make amends for any actual injury sustained. He was shocked that duellists sat in places of honor in the federal government, and to put them there was "to place ourselves under the government of the barbarian and the savage."[34]

Lyman Beecher held that the practice of duelling aroused contempt for all law; the duellist took the law into his own hands. It restrained freedom of the press and free speech, for the duellist would slay any who were likely to betray his secrets. He called upon all church members to take a vigorous stand against it, to array public opinion against those who indulged in it. Duelling could be stopped if people would only demand prompt and vigorous execution of the law, and declined to vote for any man guilty of it.[35] To vote for a duellist was to prostrate justice. Beecher carried his fight to the Long Island Presbytery in 1806.[36] Evidently he stepped on some sore toes. But he was not bothered or frightened by cries of *priestcraft* and *political preaching*.

> If we may not denounce duelling, because men of political eminence are guilty of the crime; because the enlightening of the consciences of our people would affect an election; every crime would soon find sanctuary in the example of some great politician. . . .[37]

Being a Beecher, it is more than likely that he succeeded in getting a number of his fellow ministers to sign on the dotted line, henceforth to oppose this evil, which has long since disappeared from American and English life.

We now come to that problem in society, which along with slavery, has caused more comment and resulted in more legislation, perhaps, than any other in our American life. Temperance legislation began early in this country — as early as 1642 in Maryland.[38] Yet the evils persisted. Mere boys went about drunk on the streets of our cities in 1807.[39] No wonder the first temperance society was formed at Saratoga Springs in 1808,[40] and by 1830, there were more than one thousand such local organizations in the United States.[41] Indiana, in 1832, had the distinction of enacting the first local option law, the Order of the Sons of Temperance was formed in New York City in 1842,[42] and the Washington Society, composed of reformed drinkers who had signed the pledge, was instituted in Baltimore in 1840. Before long it secured about five hundred thousand pledge signers.[43] Maine in 1851 became the first state to adopt total prohibition of intoxicants by law.[44] In passing, one may point out the parallel between the Washington Society of the 1840s and Alcoholics Anonymous of the 1940s.

Christian people were being informed about drink and intemperance. Clergymen, Unitarian and Trinitarian, as well as others, were having their say. Hearers of sermons and readers of Christian literature were being educated concerning the growth and evils of liquor consumption. "Statements Respecting Intemperance," appearing in the *Christian Disciple*, indicated that New York City had one dramshop for every fourteen persons in the city in 1819; and in the following year spent $1,893,011.00 for intoxicants of various kinds.[45] By 1860, the Rev. T. B. Thayer was telling the Warren Street Universalists, in Boston, that in the preceding year, the Police Court of their city handled 8,665 cases of which 4,300 were for drunkenness, to say nothing of instances of assault and battery and petit larceny, which everybody knew were often the results of drinking, but not listed in the court records.[46]

The scholarly William Ellery Channing, on February 28, 1837, delivered an address on the subject. This was the day appointed, when "friends of temperance throughout the world" were asked to meet in their respective communities to generate sentiment in favor of their cause. Dr. Channing had been invited by the Council of the Massachusetts Temperance Society to come to the Odeon, to speak; and here he unburdened his soul — that is, if Unitarians had souls and ever did unburden them. Temperance was a great cause, he said; one that should "animate a Christian minister."[47] They did not meet for any selfish reason, "but for the purpose of arresting a great moral and social evil."[48] It was in the interest of "promoting the virtue, dignity, [and] well-being of men" that they assembled.[49] Channing did not know that he had anything original to contribute — friends of the cause had already fully investigated the subject — yet he was not altogether sure that the essential evil had been emphasized quite so much as it should be. He was concerned with the vice, "the extent of its temptations, — its cause, — the means of its prevention and cure."[50]

Intemperance, Channing held, blinded reason; a man lost his rational and moral self under its influence, and the more he indulged in the habit the greater the degradation. To the liberal preacher all other casualties in connection with drink were of minor significance. Of course the evil debauched the mind, destroyed the body, created misery, and poverty; it added to the expense of public charity and injured the drunkard's family — all because one person became an inebriate. But all these were subordinate to that "inward ruin which he is working".[51]

Channing was eager to "awaken universal vigilance" against temptation — no sector was immune, the ignorant and the poor, the educated and the rich, the young and the old, the idle and the overworked were all exposed to it:

> Do not say that I exaggerate your exposure to intemperance. Let no man say, when he thinks of the drunkard, broken in health and spoiled of intel-- lect, "I can never so fall." He thought as little of falling in his earlier years. The promise of his youth was as bright as yours; and even after he began his downward course he was as unsuspicious as the firmest around him, and would have repelled as indignantly the admonition to beware of intemperance. The danger of this vice lies in its almost imperceptible approach.[52]

Perhaps the fault did lie with the intemperate themselves, for the most part — they should have been stronger to resist evil. But they were weak. "Still, society, by increasing temptation and diminishing men's power to resist, becomes responsible for all wide-spread vices. . . ."[53]

How should the evil be removed? "To rescue men, we must act on them inwardly and outwardly." Strengthen their ability to resist temptation. "No man is safe against this foe but he who is armed with moral force. . . ." Offset the lure of it for the poor and laboring classes by offering "them the means of intellectual, moral, and religious improvement." But the problem could not be resolved among them, if nothing were done to attack it in the upper strata, whose vices were reflected in the lower only in grosser forms. Strengthen men's moral reserves by lifting the tone of the community.[54] Remove temptation — substitute harmless and uplifting pleasures for such vicious ones. Attack ardent spirits first — banish them. Promote total abstinence. Build up a public opinion which would demand the suppression of the license system.[55]

Sympathetic to Channing's point of view, Theodore

Parker also assailed intemperance. Distressed over the sight of drunkenness in the streets, he attacked the socially and financially prominent who set a poor example: "if rich men continue to drink without need, the poor will long continue to be drunk. Vices, like decayed furniture, go down."[56] Parker thought "the refined man who often drinks, but is never drunk, corrupts hundreds of men whom he never saw, and, without intending, becomes a foe to society."[57] It was his contention that the moderate drinker was a greater promoter of drunkenness than the drunkard.

Interestingly enough, this religious pariah in the Athens of America could lament the removal of orthodox Lyman Beecher from Boston, the death of Channing and Ware, and the fact that John Pierpont was driven from his pulpit. Whatever their differences in theology, he felt they had a community of interest in denouncing a common enemy. He unhesitatingly denounced those who engaged in the manufacture and sale of liquor, especially the rich. One can almost see him standing there in Melodeon Hall, Boston, speaking with intense earnestness; a congregation equal to any drawn by Henry Ward Beecher, or Phillips Brooks (later in the century); as he raised the question: "Who of you has not lost a relative, at least a friend, in that withering flame, that terrible *auto-da-fe*, that hell-fire on earth?"[58]

Was it the orator being carried away with the music of his own voice and words before the multitude? Hardly! Parker had his facts with him. Did he not know, for example, that in the neighboring state, the then relatively small city of Albany had 633 persons in its poor-house, of whom 615 were intemperate?[59]

Some men paid a high price for their denunciation of this social evil. John Pierpont, mentioned above, was one of them. Pierpont was born near Litchfield, Connecticut, and graduated from Yale in 1804, where he taught for a time.

Then he went to Harvard to prepare for the ministry. About 1819, he succeeded Dr. Holley, at the Hollis St. Unitarian Church, Boston, where he was intsalled the pastor, and where he served popularly for twenty-five years. The remainder of his ministry was characterized by difficulties with prominent members of his parish, primarily because of his strong position against intoxicants. They were on opposite sides of the fence, and finally he was driven from his pulpit.[60]

It was more than just so much talk. Though loosely organized in their congregational systems, Unitarians could get together to battle against a social enemy. Chief among those promoting the Massachusetts Society for the Suppression of Intemperance, organized in Boston, February 5, 1813, hardly before the denomination achieved independent identity, were Channing, Abiel Abbott, Pierce, Henry Ware, Jr., and John G. Palfrey — the same who became editor of the *North American Review,* Harvard professor of history, legislator and secretary of state of Massachusetts.[61]

Orthodox Congregationalists were equally disposed to regard liquor as the arch enemy of the human race. Although Leonard Bacon could never bring himself to believe prohibition was the solution for the problem, yet he was a teetotaler in principle and preached temperance sermons.[62] His biographer suggests that some courage was required of him, as a young man, when he scored drinking as a social experience, especially a habit of such long standing and so intimately associated with hospitality. Very likely every man in his congregation served liquor in his home, and his remarks on the subject had the appearance of criticism directed toward his men. Yet what he had to say was quite fair; the evils were apparent, and, we are told, his efforts were crowned with some degree of success.[63]

More extreme, perhaps, in his views was Dr. E. N.

Kirk, the Plan of Union Presbyterian-Congregationalist, of Albany. Temperance, he thought, was connected with the cause of religion. Money used for liquor constituted wanton waste, imbibing tended to demoralise, moderate use led to immoderate use, and abstinence was essential to sobriety.[64] In another blast against the traffic, Dr. Kirk held that to sell alcohol as a beverage "is now murder in sight of God".[65] He estimated that there were approximately 500,000 drunkards in the United States; the license system was wrong, and should be abolished.[66]

The Beechers, both Lyman and Henry, were against liquor. Lyman's *Six Sermons on Intemperance* created quite a stir. He contended that a drunkard was unfit to be a legislator, and that no man of enlightened conscience could vote for him.[67] Henry said: "Every year I live increases my sober conviction that the use of intoxicating drinks is a greater destroying force to life and virtue than all other physical ills combined."[68]

Joseph Tuckerman, who saw the results of drinking there among his poor in Boston, had his views on the liquor question. With Channing and others he fought to retain a State law curtailing the sale of intoxicants, although he felt self-imposed restraints were more effective, ultimately, than legislation of a prohibitory nature. Legal measures ought not to be enacted until moral means had proven themselves incapable of meeting the problem. Tuckerman thought harsh laws might even accentuate the difficulty. He did seek the co-operation of many, including prominent persons, among whom were some public officials, to awaken conscience against putting temptation in the way of those who were weak. Toward the drinker and drunkard, he took a kindly attitude. Not only was he sympathetic, but he regarded the habit as a kind of sickness, to be treated medicinally as well as morally. His was an era which held to medication, and when he found any who impressed him as wanting to give up drinking, he went to the drugstore to procure medicine for the purpose and took it to the home of the victim. Tuckerman even went so far as to find a new environment for some young persons addicted to drink, in the hope that this would produce beneficial results.[69]

Reference has already been made to the 1,000 local temperance societies in 1830 (p. 29). Perhaps most of them were affiliated with the Protestant churches. The report of L. Farnam, missionary to Princeton, Illinois — oldest Congregational Church in the state — to the Rev. Absalom Peters, secretary of the American Home Missionary Society, indicated that the temperance society connected with his church had 140 members.[70] His report was typical, for we are told that in Western New York, there were many Congregational ministers serving Congregational and Presbyterian churches, under the Plan of Union, and that: "Almost all the ministers and members of the churches are enrolled members of Temperance Societies, and practise on the principle of total abstinence as a beverage from all intoxicating liquors."[71]

While sermons and addresses of the eastern clergy were being printed, the western missionaries were busily engaged in organizing temperance societies.[72] Hardly had Jeremiah Porter begun his assignment as a missionary to young Chicago, when he gathered a temperance society.[73] E. H. Hazard, another missionary, in a single report, told of securing twenty signers to the total abstinence pledge.[74] The Congregational Association, which met at Griggsville, Illinois, in 1838, and consisting of ministers and delegates from the churches of the State, advised: (1) total abstinence, (2) financial support for the State Temperance Society, (3) circulation of the *Temperance Herald* and other literature, (4) efforts to make it a penal offense for any candidate for public office to attempt to secure votes by means of giving drinks to prospective voters, (5) efforts to secure state-wide prohibition, and (6) that frequent meetings be held for discussion of the subject.[75]

Religious leaders wrote their convictions into the rules of the churches. For example, the Congregational Church, Du Page, Cook County, Illinois, on November 29, 1833, "*Resolved,* That the members of this church totally abstain from the manufacture, traffic & use of ardent spirits, & from furnishing them on any occasion, except for medicinal, chemical, or mechanical purposes."[76]

Whatever justification Theodore Parker may have had for saying that the churches of his day were guilty of "never rebuking a popular and profitable sin, but striking hands by turns with every popular form of wrong,"[77] it would seem that the question of drink in his day was not a vulnerable point with the Protestant clergy. The minister of the First Congregational Church, Concord, the Rev. Nathaniel Bouton, seems to have been right when he maintained that pastors were the enemies of intemperance.[78] By the 1830s, with few exceptions, it would seem that the laity were behind their preachers. The cause of temperance was marching on to victory. It would appear that denunciations of liquor, in comparison with gambling and duelling, were disproportionately numerous. However, it is well to recall that as for gambling, it was outlawed in most of the New England states, at the time; and both gambling and duelling could much more easily engage a man's occupation, especially the former, without being so easily detected by the clergy and other church members, whereas the man who drinks invariably carries with him the evidence of it. Moreover, the use of liquor was much more common than either of the other vices. Therefore, it would seem that the greater courage was required to attack the greater evil.

CHAPTER IV

CHILDREN AND WOMEN

Large families were an economic asset in frontier America, where farms were large,[1] and every home was a miniature factory. Children were expected to be useful in the young country. Calvinism, the theology of the Congregationalists, Baptists, Presbyterians, and some others, advocated work in principle, on the ground that it made for righteousness,[2] although there were definite limits to the principle, as evidenced by the Pilgrim Fathers, who among other reasons left Holland because of the burdens of urban industrial life, which rested too heavily upon their youth.[3] Yet work was one of the cardinal virtues, and every child had his duties.[4] Theodore Parker himself had to keep water buckets and wood-box filled, milk cows and feed cattle, and as he grew older he learned the use of tools, to make pumps, barrels, cider-presses and other things.[5]

If colonial America experienced a shortage of labor, matters were further complicated by the rise of the nineteenth century factory system. Workers before 1860 were recruited largely from farmers' families.[6] Children provided from 40 to 60 percent. of the total number of American factory hands in the years 1800 to 1860.[7] This meant that in every one hundred thousand factory workers, anywhere from 40,000 to 60,000 were children. Not infrequently some of them were only four years old, one year younger than we now admit them to the kindergartens in our public schools. Child labor was cheap labor,[8] and therefore child labor. In the State of Massachusetts alone, between 1820 and 1831, cotton manufacturing expanded from an annual output of seven hundred thousands dollars per year, to more than seven million dollars, an increase of more than 1,000 percent. No wonder a mill owner in 1832 complained that he was not getting enough women and children to do the work![9]

Not only was child labor an increasing problem, but so was juvenile delinquency! In 1878, F. B. Sanborn, then secretary of the American Social Science Society, praised the work accomplished by the juvenile reformatories of the United States, the first of which had been founded fifty-three years earlier in the State of New York, on Randall's Island, New York City. Edward Livingston, publicist, philanthropist and congressman, was the inspiration for this venture, and in 1826 a similar institution was opened in Boston, and one year later still another in Philadelphia.[10] Questions concerning the child's health, education, moral and spiritual training also confronted the age.

A number of religious leaders recognized, discussed and proposed their remedies for all these problems relating to childhood. A Worcester minister, the Rev. T. W. Higginson, may have felt the sting of criticism that churchmen were not interesting themselves in the socializing of Christianity. At any rate he must have been aware of some such comment, for he felt impelled to make reply, when delivering an installation sermon: *Things New and Old.* No doubt he startled staid New England by bluntly advocating radicalism in religion.[11] Then he paid his respects to his critics, or rather the critics: "To denounce them (the clergymen) and spare their rich parishioners, is to denounce the weather cock and spare the breeze that whirls it—a policy quite safe indeed, but not, perhaps, either heroic or effectual."[12] Unconsciously he was indicting his own colleagues who permitted men of wealth to color and restrain their expressions on social issues. Yet Higginson himself declined to be silenced. He knew there were social problems, among them child labor, which he specifically included in the evils of the hour. Religion, he held, should take the lead in all social reforms, even to the extent of influencing legislation.[13]

Speaking on *The Sacredness of Personality the Shield of Liberty,* the Rev. N. H. Chamberlain showed that he had made some study of child labor, both French and American, and he had come to the conclusion that weighting young lives down with hard work was both "a trespass upon the soul," and a "sin against the State".[14] American citizens should be able-bodied persons. Sickness and ignorance were the foes of freedom. So the State had a function to perform.[15] Samuel Barrett, before the congregation of the Twelfth Street Church (Unitarian), Boston, in March, 1857, preached on *Youths Void of Understanding,* in which he was very much concerned over habits of the young which were harmful to health and morals.[16] The Reverend Heman Humphrey, Congregational minister at Pittsfield, Massachusetts, as early as 1818, called attention to the unwholesome situation of housing victims of drink, prostitutes and children together.[17] Parker registered disapproval over conditions which produced 2,000 vagrants in Boston (p. 12).

Interest in education, discussed in chapter two, was in no small measure both the result of a genuine concern for the younger generation and the proposed means of meeting the needs of youth. Men like Parker (p. 12) and Chamberlain (p. 13) were persuaded that universal education would be the sure solution for evils menacing childhood.

Friendship between Parker and Charles Loring Brace may have stimulated Parker's interest in the problems of childhood. At any rate it seems indisputable that Parker learned something from Brace, of whom more will be written later. The Boston preacher called attention to the high mortality rate among the children of the poor. Something should be done for neglected children.[18] His picture of vagrancy was not very pretty.[19] He placed responsibility where it belonged—with society. Steps were advocated to deal with juvenile delinquency, and he thought the Massachusetts State Reform School for Boys was a move in the right direction.[20] But if Parker began with the cradle, his Trinitarian colleague, Edward Norris Kirk, over in Albany, was convinced that duties to childhood must be performed long before the baby was placed in its crib. He contended that something constructive must be done to educate, train, and prepare for motherhood, the poor and ignorant women, in order that they might know how to rear a family properly.[21]

What were the views of William Ellery Channing concerning children and their problems? Did he who pleaded so eloquently for temperance and peace, education and social justice, have nothing to say about children? He did speak of the duties of children to their parents.[22] His address before the Sunday School Society had been prepared and delivered with great care; and in it he posed the question: "who has not an interest in the young?"[23] To a man of Channing's integrity and sensitivity that question was tantamount to an assertion that he was vitally interested. He went on to say: "The little child is as dear to him (God), as the philosopher, as the angel . . . you must have faith in the child whom you instruct."[24] As for the doctrine of total depravity, which regarded infants as children of the devil, he refused to believe it.[25] Channing wanted Sunday School teachers to "Feel that your scholar, young as he is, is worthy of your intensest interest." They were to "have faith in the child as capable of knowing and loving the good and the true, as having a conscience to take the side of duty, as open to ingenuous motives for well-doing."[26] Great was his sympathy for the young, whose principles were exposed to fearful assaults: the rising generation was being subjected to temptations "with new violence." This was the day when society needed wise and good parents and other leaders to direct youth aright.[27] So children were the first care of the older generation; there was no better way of discharging one's obligations to society than to promote their well-being and to make them "enlightened and worthy members" of the church.[28]

Channing knew there were children "baptized into drunkenness,"[29] and that beggary was being "transmitted from parent to child".[30] He was quite aware of environment detrimental to childhood,[31] so he could speak appreciatively of his contemporary, Dr. Joseph M. Tuckerman, the minister-at-large. Tuckerman was a Harvard graduate, for twenty-five years pastor of the Unitarian Church at Chelsea. In 1826 he resigned that post in order to assume his new work in Boston.[32] So it was, in 1841, at Warren St. Chapel, where Tuckerman had done so much good, that Channing paid tribute to his efforts. This man who could not be prevented by snow, rain, wind or storms, heat or cold, pain or pleasure, from ministering to the needs of the poor and downtrodden,[33] was a great friend of the children.[34] Did he meet a begging child on the street? Time for other things had no importance. Then and there, Tuckerman had to start gathering data for his case history, not for academic reasons—no, not for that—but because of a great humanitarian passion to help.[35] The market-place, the wharf, or wherever it was that the truant went to learn his first lessons in crime, there this man of God was to be found looking for him. "He was unwearied in his efforts to place these children in schools; and multitudes owe to him their moral safety and the

education which prepared them for respectable lives."[36]
Was it necessary to send some to the House of Reformation,
which was founded in 1826? Tuckerman did not shrink
from that responsibility, but when they were released he
was on hand to welcome and to befriend them. [37] Occa-
sionally he lost patience, but not with the child. His ve-
hement denunciations were directed against negligent parents, or the social order which permitted and inculcated
unfortunate practices among children. So prevention became
a part of Tuckerman's remedy. Unprotected children of
the poor needed wholesome environment and proper direction.[38] Child welfare, opportunities for the poorest in
school, for whom he secured text-books, truancy, juvenile
delinquency were all of greatest interest to Tuckerman. He
wanted special officers to deal with truancy; the House of
Reformation he regarded as a training school, and not a
prison. To the police court and to the school he journeyed
often in behalf of his wards. He wanted no child taken
from his parents and put away in an institution, if it could
be avoided.[39] Tuckerman had a way with him when it
came to children. Over there, at Warren St. Chapel, they
came to listen to what he had to say, when they might
have been playing.[40] To him, the children and Boston were
indebted for the Farm School, for which he was the prime
mover.[41]

Joseph Tuckerman's influence was wide. In England he
met Rammohun Roy, the Hindu leader, who listened to
him with respect; and in France Baron Degerando, the
philanthropist, exchanged views with him.[42] It was no
surprise, then, that he was credited with providing the
inspiration, as professor Francis G. Peabody claimed, for
the establishment of the Boston Children's Mission, after
his death, or that John Williams, a Unitarian layman, became its first president.[43] Or that Charles Barnard carried
on children's aid work at Warren St. Chapel.[44]

Two more names must be added to those already mentioned. There was Horace Bushnell, whose indirect influence far outweighed his direct achievements in behalf of children. A love for children must have been interwoven with his distress over Hartford slums and his advocacy of the public park to replace that awful sore spot in the city,[45] and his *Christian Nurture,* the book which came to be so popular in Christian circles, surely awakened considerable interest in children on the part of his readers. Here he advocated the environment and teaching which would bring up a child with no other awareness than that he was a Christian and a child of God.[46]

Bushnell was the spiritual father to Charles Loring Brace. A member of the former's Hartford parish in his boyhood, Brace never forgot that privilege and paid high tribute to his childhood minister.[47] Born in Litchfield, Connecticut, Brace graduated from Yale College in 1846, continued his studies in Yale Divinity School for the next two years, and in the following year graduated from Union Theological Seminary. His entire life was devoted to the poor of New York, even as Tuckerman gave himself to similar classes in Boston, and like the latter he too gained international fame in his chosen work. In 1852 he began to hold meetings for boys, and in the following year founded the Children's Aid Society. His interest in newsboys prompted him to start lodging-houses, workshops and industrial schools for them.[48] In addition to cheap lodging houses and industrial schools, he also advocated night schools, summer camps and sanitoria.[49] Brace published *The Best Method of Disposing of Our Pauper and Vagrant Children* in 1859. [50]

Children and Women, women and children. Somehow the two go together in our minds. So it is natural to turn from the needs and problems of childhood to the question of woman, her sphere, her rights and her responsibilities. Perhaps it was Brattle St. Church, Boston, organized in 1669, and which was the liberal fly in orthodox ointment, which was responsible for it all.[51] It was to be expected that the fly, being liberal, would surely do an unheard of thing. The Church accepted the Westminster Confession as the basis of its beliefs, but loosely interpreted, and *from the beginning women were permitted a voice in its affairs,*[52] although women did not sit in a Unitarian Convention until 1865.[53]

Originally none of the thirteen charter states to compose the Federal Union explicitly restricted suffrage to the men. New York was the first to do so, acting in 1778; and New Jersey was the last, passing its restrictive measures in 1844.[54] It is difficult to say what was the primary factor in awakening churchmen to an interest in woman's rights. Certainly it does seem that other matters than the subject itself were responsible for it.[55] Working conditions, children, slavery and education all seem to have played an important part, as did also prostitution. As early as 1830, Joseph Tuckerman concerned with the causes of poverty among Boston's underprivileged, discovered that a considerable number of them were poor because of inadequate wages and lack of employment. His studies led him straight into the factories of New England, where so many women and children worked, and he learned that the women were not paid enough. So low wages were responsible for the unhappiness and immorality in families of the poor. The situation was such as to force women to choose between hunger and want on the one hand, or prostitution on the other.[56] One manufacturer told Tuckerman that he had fifty applications a day from women to make shirts of coarse material, for from $6\frac{1}{4}$ to 10 cents per day. Many of them worked for $1.25 per week, had but two to three days of employment in the average week, and paid as much as $1.00 a week for a bare room without a bed; $1.25 with a bed.[57]

Women had almost exclusive influence over children in the first fifteen years of their life. So "the elevation of woman in America" became "one of the most interesting social problems" to the Rev. A. D. Mayo, of Cleveland, Ohio.[58] Channing exerted profound influence in awakening not a little interest in this concern for a larger sphere for woman. He laid heavy responsibility on women for social advancement. Slavery seems to have been the issue with which he associated the women, to them he committed the cause of the enslaved.[59] When reminded that women in the anti-slavery crusade would take them out of their natural sphere, he questioned: "What, let me ask, is woman's work."[60] They were "to sympathize with human misery" and "to keep alive in society some feeling of human brotherhood."[61] If the home was to be the scene of woman's most important activities, it must not restrict her interests and compassions to four walls. Indeed Channing strongly suggested that such a narrow place, which shuts out "the principles of universal justice and universal charity" might well be deserted—in fact it was almost incumbent upon a Christian woman to leave that type of domicile in order to perform her real and larger duties.[62] Channing may well have provoked and awakened many New England women to a new awareness of their place in human society, for he was, as we know, one of the outstanding divines of his generation—a Unitarian among the very Unitarians who became leaders in asserting woman's rights: Elizabeth Cady Stanton, Susan B. Anthony, Lucy Stone, Julia Ward Howe, Mary A. Livermore, Margaret Fuller, Maria Weston Chapman, Caroline H. Dull, and Louisa M. Alcott.[63]

Their zeal for education led not a few of the New England clergy to become the advocates of universal schooling, with opportunities for all. Commitment to education for everybody included women. So men like Ezra S. Gannett, Lemuel Capen and Samuel May took their stand (p. 17). Gannett held the position that woman's place was not what it should be in a Christian society:

> Questions in regard to property, education, employment, and the control of her own powers and of others, which have in ages past been settled by a blind and arrogant prescription, must now be examined frankly, candidly, and thoroughly; and the result must be a relinquishment of many notions of which we speak mildly when we pronounce them venerable mistakes.[64]

Orville Dewey, of New York, used the term "woman's rights," even though some persons might not like it.[65] Woman had suffered great wrongs and was entitled to justice; the word *obey* should be dropped from the marriage ceremony. A wife might be a silent partner in the marriage contract, but a partner nevertheless. No drunken husband had a right to take his wife's earnings for his vice; checks were needed on the powers of an improvident and/or vicious mate. A woman had as much right to and need for education as a man. He thought the very idea of any difference in the intellect of the sexes was absurd; however, he was not ready to have a woman go into business or have the ballot.[66]

Long before Dewey expressed his views, the Rev. Elias Gilbert, preaching at Greenfield, on July 4, 1810, chose as his subject: *Civil and Religious Liberty, Precious and Worth Preserving*. In this address he did not deny the right of the ballot to woman, but he did exclude her from office-holding and soldiering. However, he exhorted the feminine part of his congregation "to promote knowledge, true virtue and patriotism," and to his larger audience he said: "Never think that woman was made to stand as a mere cypher in the community."[67]

It was to be expected that Dr. Rufus Anderson, speaking at the second anniversary of the opening of Mt. Holyoke Female Seminary (College), July 24, 1839, should have something to say about women and their training. He thought female education was still on trial; he pleaded for it and deplored the prejudice against it. Ignorance would not fit a woman for her sphere. Since she exerted a commanding influence on human character, she required the best.[68] Among the things he hoped for and expected was the development of physical education, in order that there might be more healthful women.[69] Apparently the Rev. A. D. Mayo, of Cleveland was ready to go further than Anderson, or many of the others, in this matter of woman's rights. Seemingly he wished to go the entire way, and let her vote, hold office, and be admitted to all activities open to men. At any rate, he held that: "It is an outrage to the common sense of mankind to say that woman in America does not require a larger field of labor". She should have "a better opportunity for culture". The time was at hand for "a more direct voice in public affairs than she has enjoyed in the social organizations of the old world."[70]

Perhaps the most dangerous enemy of any plan to ameliorate a social ill or injustice is the individual who, having genuine social vision, voices his oppositon from deep-seated convictions that he is acting in the best interests of society and the particular group for whom the plan is advanced. At any rate Horace Bushnell, truly great socializer in many respects, was the opponent of woman's suffrage on the ground that it would injure the home and coarsen woman. He foresaw the fact that it would "make our ladies mere women to us . . ."[71] So keenly did he feel about it, that in 1869, somewhat later than our period, he published *Women's Suffrage; the Reform Against Nature.* Whether his wife agreed or not, we do not know, yet he dedicated the volume to her.[72] Bushnell believed wholeheartedly in co-education. Woman's presence on the campus would have a sanitizing influence on "the ancient, traditional hell-state of college life, and all the immense ruin of character propagated by the club-law of a stringently male or monastic association."[73] He saw the professions opening up to women, which was right; the disabilities had been wrong. Apparently he was even willing for them to engage professionally in religious work. Some doors he thought would always be closed to them, such as agriculture, engineering and war. [74] But woman's suffrage! No! If that dreadful thing should come to pass, he thought, "our sun is set; is there any other sun to rise?"[75] Could it have been that Horace was a *Republican,* and his wife a *Democrat,* or vice versa? The reason he gave, and which he most likely believed with heart and soul was that it would strike at the heart of the institution of marriage and the home.[76] Would political differences split the family? Would it injure domestic life, if both husband and wife attended political mass meetings in a day that had no foreknowledge of the radio to come? Perhaps he feared it.

But that other annoyance to the reverend gentleman of New England, Theodore Parker, anticipated the day when woman should be raised from the status of subordinate and property of, to the equal of man, and he looked for "peaceful, blessed consequences".[77] Domestic duties did not exhaust all of a woman's powers. Her functions, like charity, began at home; and then, like charity, went everywhere. To confine women to domestic duties constituted, in his judgment, "monstrous waste".[78] The number of unmarried women was increasing; he did not think it would be a permanent situation, but it had to be considered. There were three classes of women he found; (1) domestic drudges who were decreasing in number; (2) dolls who wanted to be ornaments and therefore hated the elevation of woman; and (3) the women who performed their domestic duties, who were both useful and ornamental, plus much more.[79] Modern invention was decreasing the amount of work to be done in the home, leaving time for other activities.[80] So he asked: Who would want a Jenny Lind to be a housekeeper and nothing more? Many women had no talent for housework, but were fitted for other things. Should they be relegated to uselessness? What about young women engaged to be married and whose marriage was somewhat deferred? Should they be useless until married?[81] What were women to do? Intellectual pursuits, that is, learning for learning's sake only, was open to relatively few—not by reason of outside pressure, but because of natural limitations as to ability along those lines. There were the practical outlets, which included domestic work, mechanical labor, trade and teaching. But these were not enough. If a woman was a human being, then she possessed the nature and rights of a human being.[82] She had a right to develop her human nature, and to enjoy her human rights, and to perform her human duties.[83] She was to have the same rights as a man.[84] True, woman's education was making progress, but it was necessary to go much farther.[85] Woman should take her place on the public platform and enter the professions of medicine, law and theology.[86] Woman had a right to equal suffrage with man, and should have it. If half of the political offices in Boston were held by the women, he thought it would be a better city, with improved government.[87] Woman might never take so much interest in politics as man, but that was for the women to decide, and not the men.[88]

Whether Joseph Tuckerman was interested in woman's

suffrage, his biographer does not seem to indicate.[89] But he was interested in their wages, and he won the one hundred dollar prize for writing the winning essay on the subject.[90] He was the friend of unfortunate and helpless women. To the House of Correction he went to talk with them; he brought about some reform at the Female Asylum. No doubt he had a word of comfort for unhappy mothers who came to the place where he was to talk with some boys who had been guilty of stealing. A poor woman, with millinery experience, needed money, so he solicited his friends for funds to set her up in business.[91]

Closely allied with, indeed a part of the woman question was prostitution. A deplorable situation existed. While the evil itself is more ancient than history, apparently there never will be anything like an accurate history of the subject, for comparatively few men write their memoirs and fewer still have included their illicit sex experiences in their autobiographies; and certainly the women will not tell in any considerable numbers. But according to one authority, the first attempted exhaustive survey of prostitution took place in New York City in 1855, at the instigation of Dr. W. W. Sanger, under the auspices of the city police force. A questionnaire was filled out by 2,000 prostitutes.[92] The population of the city at that time, we estimate, was about 800,000—one of these unfortunate women to every 400 persons. More than twenty years earlier, *McDowall's Journal,* a monthly publication devoted to the cause of moral reform, was published in New York, which contained some enlightening information, if not edifying. Either the situation had improved radically by the time the police made their survey, or their data was hopelessly inadequate, or, indeed, previous figures may have been too high. But we are advised that in 1816, when the city's population stood at about 120,000 inhabitants, the number of prostitutes was placed at 8,000, or one for every 15 persons, which does seem to be unusually large. To be sure one must take into account the fact that New York was a port of entry, and as such had a large floating male population. By 1833, the New York Magdalene Society reported not fewer than 10,000 of them i.e. prostitutes in that city.[93] Boston, too, had its unfortunate women of the street. The *Journal* described Kimball House, an elegantly furnished brothel of four stories, located on Gore Street, and in operation for seventeen years.[94]

William Ellery Channing touched upon the subject in speaking of the evils of slavery. He thought the institution made illicit sex relations inevitable.[95] Both slaves and owners were being robbed of homes entitled to rightful purity. Half-breed children born of these unholy alliances appalled him, and he was horrified that their white fathers sold them into slavery.[96] Channing might speak of the evils of immortality south of the Mason and Dixon line, but not Theodore Parker, not so long as the presence of 200 brothels in Boston haunted him,[97] and while he was having his say in the capital of Massachusetts, his neighbor, Kirk, in the capital of New York, was also relieving his mind. Kirk insisted that something must be done to rehabilitate these women of the street and brothel. Each was certain that some honest effort should be made to prevent further recruiting of women for such purposes.[98] The inequality of woman was, in Parker's opinion, an underlying cause for prostitution.[99] While Kirk had implicit faith in education as the panacea for this wrong, Parker apparently countenanced incontinence under certain circumstances,[100] to which Dr. Richard C. Cabot, of Harvard Medical School, in a later day, disagreed.[101]

Yet it was Parker who had the greatest sympathy for, the largest understanding of, and the kindliest feeling toward the woman, who for one reason or another descended to that low level of existence. He understood and spoke against the vows of celibate nuns and priests in the Roman Catholic Church.[102]

The questions of woman and sex were closely associated with that of divorce. Historically Christianity has been against divorce on the basis of Christ's meager teaching (Mt. 5.32, Mk. 10.4), which is also indecisive, or at least open to question. Here in the United States statistics seem to be entirely lacking for the years prior to 1887. Theodore Dwight Woolsey, who was licensed to preach in 1825 and who became president of Yale in 1846, was a contemporary of many of the men quoted in these pages. When he became interested in the subject we do not know; it was not until 1882 that he wrote *Divorce and Divorce Legislation*, which went through many editions.[103] In view of the fact that Parker made notes on the subject, it is not unlikely that Woolsey himself had some inkling of what was going on in this respect long before writing his book. Parker saw the mounting tide of legal separation and the causes challenged him. What were those underlying reasons which resulted in the disintegration of the home? Were there good people who married for pure reasons, who later discovered a tragic mistake had been made, Physiological and psychological factors worked to prevent a happy marriage. That was disastrous. But what could be done about it? Perhaps liberalization of the laws governing divorce might help; he wasn't sure; and not having proved to his own mind that he had the solution was excellent reason for him not to say too much about it.[104] He supposed that the Greeks could add something to the Christian concept of morality and woman, thereby improving the situation; and of this he was fairly certain, that the correct view of marriage and divorce could not be attained until men arrived at the correct idea concerning the status of woman.[105]

Practical steps were taken toward the elevation of woman, in each of which the clergy, that is some of them, and the church, in part, had a share. In the period under discussion, great incentives to woman's education were offered. Academies and woman's colleges, and co-education became a fact. Mt. Holyoke College, as a Seminary, opened its doors in the 1830s.[106] Oberlin afforded equal opportunities to women. Lucy Stone, pioneer in woman's rights, graduated from the latter institution in 1847; so did Antoinette Blackwell, who became one of America's first ordained clergymen, of her sex, in the Orthodox Congregational ministry, and later she entered the Unitarian fellowship.[107] The Rev. Charles Finney did his part to prepare women for the larger sphere, for both of these young women were his students.[108]

Something was done, too, to remedy, if not to solve, the baneful results of prostitution. There in Boston, Parker, Phillips, Henry Bowditch and Edward Beecher established a rescue mission for girls; there they were taught how to do housework, and they were then placed in respectable homes. A Unitarian clergyman was employed as secretary of the mission.[109] *McDowall's Journal,* already alluded to (p.   ), was published in order to acquaint Christian people with conditions and to enlist their interest and support. J. R. McDowall, a clergyman, was a leader in the reform movement. He called a meeting of sympathetic persons at his own home in New York City, in 1832, to do something about it. Free Congregational Church, New Haven, contributed $10.00, less than one month after this meeting. This was done at the suggestion of a faculty member of Yale Divinity School, and Samuel Griswold, the pastor, wrote approvingly of the work and the decision to support it.[110] Magdalene Societies were formed for the purpose of rescue   work.[111]

The call for the first Woman's Rights Convention resulted in such a meeting at Worcester, Mass., October 23, 1850.[112] Ralph Waldo Emerson, who had been a Unitarian clergyman, was one of the signers to call it. Other Unitarians were Alcott, Higginson, Pillsbury, S. J. May, and W. H. Channing, nephew of William Ellery, and some others.[113] More than half of the signers of the petition, asking the Massachusetts State Legislature, in 1855, to grant women the ballot, were Unitarians.[114]

Thus, we see that though the beginnings were modest and the accomplishments as yet few, the New England clergy, or an important minority, demonstrated their interest in the cause of children and women, and started in motion the forces which were to spread and to gain ground and to make progress toward the protection of the former and the emancipation of the latter.

CHAPTER V

PHILANTHROPY, HOUSING, HEALTH AND AMUSEMENTS

Charity, as old as the Christian Church, and older, had its place in the thinking and deeds of the New England clergy of the early half of the nineteenth century. Perhaps a new emphasis made its appearance, but the interest was still there.[1] We are told that the nineteenth century ushered in reforms, systematizing, co-ordinating and improving methods of relief.[2] In the summer of 1944, the bulletin board outside famous Park St. Church, Boston, known as "Brimstone Corner", contained an impressive list of reform movements born in that historic place of worship, indicating that the Standing Order, or Established Congregational Churches of Massachusetts, played a significant part in the progressive social action of the day. Congregationalism was established in the Bay State until 1834 and in Connecticut till 1818.[3] Large numbers of prominent persons in public life and leading private citizens were members either of the Congregational or Unitarian churches. Hence almost any movement which received the representative support of the people was bound to have some members of these two denominations behind them.

The Rev. William Alger, of Roxbury, drew *Inferences from the Pestilence and Fast,* when he delivered his sermon on August 3, 1849. Cholera was a visitation of divine wrath against sinful men who ought to repent. So he felt moved to "rub it in" as we in our modern day might say. He saw: "The pitiless indifference, pride, and sloth of those who dwell in palaces, monopolizing the splendid advantages and the outward pleasures of the world, and doing nothing to make it better . . ." They deserved "to be rebuked with pain and terror . . ." If he could not produce the pain, he would do his best to furnish the terror, at least to make them uncomfortable in their complacency, for he drew his picture, for their benefit, of "The condition of the degraded and oppressed poor—humanity's orphan children, cradled in misery, baptized in tears, surrounded by squalor, brought up with abuse, neglect, and crime . . ." These unfortunates were "loaded with contempt, and avoided by the haughty heirs of rank and refinement . . ." They were "bowed down by crushing toil, enfeebled by hunger, drained of nervous life and recuperative energy by despair . . ." This, he contended, was "the deep crime and the rooted curse of mankind, and it calls aloud to God for redress."[4]

Horace Bushnell, too, knew about "hungry, shivering children crying at the door for bread . . ."[5] Caleb Stetson, of Medford, speaking to his own congregation, at the Annual Fast, April 7, 1842, was primarily concerned with slavery, but he was aware that, "If one member [of society] suffer, all the members suffer with it."[6] Poverty was not individual entirely, it had its social repercussions too. Thus, the Rev. B. R. Allen, of Salem, had discovered that God created man with a social nature, and placed him in a social state; the world was a unit, and mankind was one family (a fact which men still stubbornly refuse to accept, with resultant clashes between classes, nations and races).[7] In such a society, practical Christianity never shrinks from its duty, and never considers the duty too difficult. Christianity was obligated to wipe out the sorrows and sufferings of mankind.[8] So the Rev. Mr. Allen knew that by being benevolent, Christians justified their existence and fulfilled the will of God.[9]

Leonard Woods, the Andover professor, when invited

to conduct funeral services for the wealthy Moses Brown, a patron of the Seminary, did not think it at all inappropriate to discuss the *Duties of the Rich* before those who came to honor the memory of Brown with their presence, among whom were undoubtedly a considerable number of well-to-do. He contended for some sort of instruction to men of wealth in regard to their duty in good works. Civil laws might make the property of the rich their own, but religiously and ethically they were only God's stewards.[10]

Christianity Applied to Our Social and Civil Duties was written by the Rev. Hubbard Winslow, who had served parishes in Dover, Boston, Geneva (New York), and New York City. This was in 1835, when he asked that a real effort be made "to open wide the flood-gates of Christian benevolences . . ."[11] Conditions in the panic year, 1837, distressed Leonard Bacon, of New Haven. Perhaps his position of leadership caused many to confide in him their state of affairs. He who had his own difficulties making ends meet, on his Centre Church salary,[12] had compassion for the needy. Carefully he examined the situation, and tried to account for the depression which wrought so much havoc. Bacon became convinced that every man should have a job and wages. Apparently he would have favored a Works Progress Administration had it been offered in his time, or even a government dole, for while employment was the ideal, he held that "employment or no employment, the hungry must have bread."[13] This, too, was the attitude of Dr. Henry Bellows, there in New York City, where he reminded his congregation of the horrid state of poverty-stricken persons, their pitifully small reserves gone, now faced with distress and need. So he asked his parishioners to give generously and even sacrifically to the Association for the Improvement of Conditions among the Poor.[14] Bacon took the position that society endangered itself, if it did nothing, when suffering begets despair. So he advised the privileged classes to retrench on their luxuries and to continue their benevolences.[15]

William Ellery Channing heard: "A louder and louder cry is beginning to break forth through the civilized world for a social reform, which shall reach the most depressed ranks of the community."[16] Channing was among those who had earned the right to speak out for the depressed poor and their needs. Did not he and his friend and deacon, Jonathan Phillips, visit the poor of his parish regularly? It is related that two elderly women, in his church, were also unfortunate enough to be mentally unbalanced, and were obsessed with the idea that all their food was poisoned, if not administered by Channing or Phillips. So, for a number of years, these two men, by doing it alternately, made daily visits to them to supply their needs.[17] The Rev. Joseph Tuckerman insisted that young men ordained to the ministry were to serve the underprivileged. Christianity had done more than any other institution, not merely by establishing hospitals, alms-houses, and moving individuals to practice charity, but by recognizing the poor and needy as men, not brutes. He knew, that poverty and vice existed in the Christian era, but not because they were the fruits of the Christian faith—rather the fruits of anti-Christian forces.[18] Tuckerman as Unitarian Minister-at-Large, in Boston, became the denomination's outstanding servant of the poor, and under his leadership The Benevolent Fraternity of Unitarian Churches in the City of Boston was founded in 1834 to carry on the work.[19] To appreciate Tuckerman's work, one must read Father D. T. McColgan's biography of the man. His chapter on charity privately administered or relief publicly given tells an interesting and enlightening story, how Tuckerman's concern was so continuously for the poor that even some persons of humanitarian ideals resented him,[20] how he was painstaking in his reports, how he made many and excellent suggestions for remedial action,[21] how he sought institutional reforms,[22] and how he served as an overseer to Boston's poor.[23]

Nathaniel Bouton, of New Hampshire, preaching in 1862, two years after the close of our period, made some comparisons in the activities of the Concord Female Charitable Society. For the decade, 1812 to 1822, he learned that the Society had contributed the sum of $35.31 as an average for each of the ten years, whereas from 1852 to 1862 the average yearly sum given was $282.49.[24] Others, too, had reason to rejoice in the benevolence of Christian church members. In his *Memoirs*, Charles G. Finney spoke of Arthur Tappan's generosity. His heart, Finney said, "was as large as all New York, and I might say, as large as the world."[25] Finney whose Oberlin community and school benefited so much by Tappan's gifts had reason to know whereof he wrote. Nor were Tappan's contributions of one dimension only—they reached in every direction.[26] So, too, were the deeds of Moses Brown. The Rev. Abiel Abbott was able to transcend Unitarian lines and to pay tribute to Trinitarian Brown. Said he, "The poor have found in him, at all times, a merciful friend, and peculiarly liberal in those years of deep distress, which deranged their employments, and choked the channels of their subsistence."[27] He, too, gave to many causes.[28] It appeared that the preaching of the New England divines struck a benevolent response in the hearts of their hearers.

Yet there was a note of questioning. Was it merely the duty of the Church and its members to take compassion on those wounded along the Jericho road, apply oil and wine, and bind up the travellers' wounds, and pay for their care? Or did it become the Church's responsibility to go after the robbers?[29] The needs of the poor must be met thought Unitarian William H. Furness: "The great voice of Hu-

manity, speaking in every heart, pleads for those who are
ready to perish from hunger and cold."[30] But this matter
of giving aid required the greatest discretion . . . without
taking from . . . [the poor] what is more precious than
anything we can bestow, their self-independence."[31]

John Emery Abbot, sure that there would always be a
place for Christian charity,[32] was concerned, however, lest
indiscriminate giving breed further improvidence.[33] Others
apparently agreed with him. Among them was the Rev.
Heman Humphrey, of Pittsfield, who, speaking "On Doing
Good to the Poor," thought public institutions had a way
of putting a premium on "indolence, improvidence and
vice . . ." Society waited until individuals became the victims of poverty before doing anything about it. He was
for finding out the causes of poverty and ways and means
of preventing it.[34] As usual Theodore Parker, too, had his
opinion. He did not think the poor so much wanted "your
gold, your bread, or your cloth," as they wanted "your
sympathy, respect, and counsel," for what they really needed
was to be aided in order to help themselves. They had a
right to their own gold, by their own industry, and not be
compelled to throw themselves on the benevolence of the
affluent. "It is justice more than charity they ask." Poverty
became a condemnation of society itself, for "Every beg-
gar, every pauper, born and bred amongst us, is a re-
proach to us, and condemns our civilization." He wanted
to know why it was that here in a land of plenty, there
were men, "for no fault of their own, born into want, living
in want, and dying of want?" How could this be in a
country which professed religion, which advocated the
brotherhood of man. It struck him that there was "a hor-
rible wrong somewhere."[35]

Where there is dire poverty and need, one is almost certain to find wretched housing. But prior to the Civil War,

America was largely agrarian. In 1800 less than 4 percent. of our population was urban; and in 1860, less than 17 percent., and in 1900, less than 33 percent.[36] Under such circumstances a major part of the American people probably knew very little about overcrowded conditions in the city slum. Since gas, furnaces, running water, baths and electricity were not generally known until long after the War between the States, perhaps housing as a problem was something quite different then than now. At any rate the contrast between the houses of the rich and poor did not so much consist in the presence or absence of certain mechanical devices known to our generation. As a general rule frontier cabins were crude, one-room affairs, expanded as the family and family-treasure grew. Yet men were conscious of differences in housing. The Rev. Jeremiah Porter, writing, in August, 1831, from Sault Ste. Marie, described the comforts of the Henry R. Schoolcraft home, in which he lived.[37] Indeed, it is surprising how much was known about the housing situation.

Lawrence Veiller made a report of New York City's Housing between the years 1834 and 1900, in which he stated that Dr. John H. Griscom, the city inspector for the Board of Health, was the first to offer a comprehnsive picture of the housing conditions among the city's poor. It is appalling and almost unbelievable that in 1842, there were 1,459 cellars, in New York, inhabited by 7,196 persons for practically permanent residence. 6,618 families were living in courts or rear buildings. Immorality and disease flourished. Griscom wanted the municipal government to forbid the use of cellars for dwellings; he asked that owners and agents be required to keep inside and outside premises clean, and he wanted a law to prohibit overcrowding. But in 1846, the Association for Improving the Condition of the Poor, which was organized in 1843, took up the question of housing, and did not complete its report of fifty-three pages until 1853. In 1850, they discovered some 18,456 persons were crowded into 3,742 cellars. The Committee recommended that capitalists and real estate men erect modern tenements — they held that pure air, light and water were indispensable to good health; where these were lacking the law should close the buildings or demand remodelling.[38]

Naturally the question arises: Were any of the New England clergy aware of this situation, which placed the poor in dark, overcrowded, insanitary and unhealthful dwelling places? Unequivocally, the answer is: that some of the most eminent were fully conscious, spoke out against this condition, and advocated measures for reform. There was the Rev. Samuel J. May, prominent in many reforms, who denounced "miserable shanties of the poor,"[39] and Joseph Tuckerman knew, for he visited "the poorest hovels" in Boston.[40] The slum area of Hartford, Connecticut, was an eyesore to Dr. Horace Bushnell. Its awful tenements were a crying shame. He not only spoke his mind about it, he harped on it, he hounded city officials and others, until he got what he wanted—a park for public use in its place, and better living conditions for the inhabitants of the rookeries.[41]

Theodore Parker could describe housing conditions and blast against them. There they were, in Boston — places "without comfort or convenience, without sun, or air, or water; damp, cold, filthy, and crowded to excess. In one section of the city there are thirty-seven persons on an average to each house."[42] For the unenviable privilege of living in squalor, the poor paid the highest rental, proportionately; the houses themselves were worth nothing, the land alone was valued. He estimated that in many instances they were charged from 12 to 15 percent per year on a large valuation.[43] Nor was it the orator being carried away with his message, prone to exaggeration! Joseph Tuckerman, who knew, stated that many women worked for $1.25 per week, while the common price of a room was $1.00 per week without a bed — the latter cost an additional quarter.[44]

No wonder that the sympathetic Channing spoke not once, but many times on housing! He made it seem a shameful thing for any intelligent person not to know the conditions under which the poor lived. They would learn useful lessons and possess "holier feelings," if they would only "penetrate the dens of want, and woe, and crime, a few steps from their own door".[45] So many never saw "the damp cellar where childhood and old age spend day and night, winter and summer," so many never climbed to an upper room "which contains within its narrow and naked walls not one, but two or even three families."[46] He reminded the affluent and comfort-loving that within "the neighborhood of your comfortable or splendid dwellings are these abodes of squalid misery, of reckless crime, of bestial intemperance, of half-famished children, of dissoluteness, of temptation for thoughtless youth."[47] It was all very well and good Christianity to send supplies to the poor man's house, when he is in need; but that wasn't the way to solve the problem permanently. It wasn't primarily a matter of relieving indigence, but to dry up the sources.[48] Thus Channing became the advocate of better housing. Again and again he came back to "the filth, darkness, and dampness of their dwellings".[49] To the clergy, Channing said: "You must not wait for the poor in church. Go where no other will go. Let no squalidness, or misery, or crime, repel you."[50] The minister was to go to "the bleak room open to the winter's wind".[51] He wanted laws which would prohibit letting apartments unfit for human habitation. A place which was not properly ventilated was injurious to health. Alleys must be kept clean and an abundance of pure water provided. These would add to the health and self-respect of the poor.[52] He had other proposals too, for preventing a family from being "crowded into a single and often narrow apartment [single room], which must answer at once the ends of a parlor, kitchen, bed-room, nursery, and hospital. . . ."[53] In such an environment, it was difficult to maintain neatness, comfort and the decencies of life.[54] Here people could easily cease to respect one another, and so often the poor man was compelled to choose between "his close room and the narrow street. . . ."[55] Channing wanted a housing commissioner just the same as the city had its market commissioner. The latter prevented the sale of tainted meat and decayed vegetables, which were injurious to physical well-being. So the former, if appointed, would be obligated to prevent the rental of unfit rooms, with their putrid air, which were also a menace to the public health.[56]

Bushnell was not the only Trinitarian who wanted better housing and better cities. Speaking on *The Voice of God in the Storm*, the Rev. Joseph G. Wilson thought something was wrong with our cities. God intended men to have pure air, good water and enough room. Overcrowding, impure air and water created disease and corrupted morals. Cities should be spread out to allow for forests, parks and gardens; swamps should be drained; houses should be constructed with an eye to health and comfort; yards should be large. In short he was an advocate of city-planning, he wanted a model city.[57]

In close alliance with poverty and bad housing, and a result of both was illness. Public health was a matter of concern to everyone. Were the New England clergy aware and interested? It is a significant fact that Congregationalism and Unitarianism, for all their emphasis on social issues (at this stage in our study, we feel justified in making this assertion), did not found any hospitals. Perhaps the answer lies in the fact that they believed Christian education to be a panacea for such ills. Create in the Church enlightened members, including an educated mind and a social conscience, and those members would take the lead in the community in establishing such institutions. If this is not the answer, then there seems to be none, for other well known American religious bodies have their charitable organizations, some of which must have come into existence in this period.[58] Of course one must point out that Congregationalism, under the auspices of its American Board of Commissioners for Foreign Missions, has founded and maintains many hospitals in foreign lands.[59]

Absence of these institutions does not presuppose indifference to the physical well-being of the people. However it would be unfair to expect too much from the socializers of Christianity in the pre-Civil War era, when we recall that the American Public Health Association was not organized until 1872. Yet Bellevue Hospital, New York City, opened its doors in 1817,[60] and Boston had its Massachusetts General Hospital six years earlier; while its Lying-in Hospital began to function in 1832, and its hospital for the Insane was established in 1839.[61] Disease and health, to be sure, are not denominational affairs, but common to all humanity, and it may, indeed, be that Congregationalists and Unitarians played a significant part in the establishment of the above-mentioned institutions.

A number of the clergy were concerned with the health of the people. Joseph Tuckerman, whose father was one of the founders of Massachusetts General Hospital,[62] did not hesitate to make appointment with Dr. Walter Channing, of that institution, in an endeavor to secure free treatment for a needy person.[63] Timothy Dwight, second of that name to be president of Yale, recognized that among other evils in the world, there were enemies of public health, such as infant mortality, disease, famine and hunger.[64] While Henry Ward Beecher thought more attention should be given the subject of public health. Physiology should be taught and studied, the Young Men's Christian Association had a solemn obligation to lead in a crusade for health among men. Health was dependent upon wholesome treatment of the body. Play could be beneficial and it was up to Christian young men to lead the way.[65] The Rev. N. H. Chamberlain, of Canton, Massachusetts, was among those who saw in illness an enemy of freedom, and who believed that healthful working conditions were a requirement if a free people were to survive.[66] Dr. Henry Bellows, of New York, who did direct work with the Sanitary Commission in the Civil War, had his views too, which he shared with others. In his opinion the moral and spiritual interests of the community were tied up with public health. Disease had a way of demoralizing people. He knew the secret to good health. Give a community clean streets, abundant pure water, good sewage, parks, well--lighted, ventilated places of residence, and cheap means of getting to the country; give the people innocent amusements within reach of all and inexpensive bread. These would make a healthy and virtuous and happy neighborhood.[67] Startling, but true! in a day when women had limbs, not legs, and when nice people supposedly were too Victorian to mention sex in polite society, Bellows did the unusual thing — he wrote a book which related to a most important aspect of public health: *The Treatment of Social Diseases* (1857).[68]

Perhaps it was his own ill-health, which led Channing to place such high value on good health. At any rate he lamented the ignorance of the working classes regarding its value. It was the laborer's fortune, and he ought to guard it even more carefully than the rich man does his investments. Burdens of body and mind were lessened by the presence of good health, and increased a man's capacity for work. The sick man produces less because the task exhausts his limited supply of strength, and thereby reduces his earning capacity.[69] Dr. Channing praised the public press for making available, at little expense, knowledge concerning "the structure, and functions, and laws of the human body," which, once generally known, would make the masses conscious of the fact that disease is no accident, but "has fixed causes, many of which they can avert, and a great amount of suffering, want, and consequent intellectual depression will be removed. . . ."[70] He thought, if the public were more enlightened on the subject, people would demand effectual means of keeping the city clean, of providing pure water available to all, and of eliminating unhealthful housing conditions.[71] Although the Pure Food and Drug Act, enacted by Congress, did not go into effect until January 1, 1907,[72] it is interesting to note that Channing, in 1838, lamented the fact that newspapers in their "advertising columns were very much devoted to patent medicines. . . ."[73] They were designed to seduce the working man into buying them, and of their pernicious effect on health, he had no doubts.[74]

In addition to general health, the deaf, blind and insane came in for their share of attention. The Unitarians had a splendid part in this work. Dr. Samuel G. Howe, familiar with such service in Europe, did pioneer work among the deaf and blind in America, opening the Massachusetts School for the Blind in 1832. Howe also did valuable service for the feeble-minded.[75] Howe was a layman and a physician, husband of Julia Ward Howe, author of "The Battle Hymn of the Republic". He was also intimately associated with Theodore Parker and other New England reformers.[76] Dorothy Dix, another Unitarian, won the support and sympathy of Howe, Channing, Horace Mann and John G. Palfrey, the historian in her efforts to care for the insane.[77] Tuckerman, who also sought medical aid for persons addicted to drink, bombarded the Governor of Massachusetts with letters, pleading for better treatment of the unfortunate mentally sick.[78]

There were those who saw a place in the scheme of things for good recreation. When the Rev. Joseph G. Wilson asked for "forests, parks, gardens . . . [and] larger yards,"[79] he undoubtedly expected people to enjoy them. Horace Bushnell rejoiced in wholesome play. He thought there were abundant games, but those most beneficial were of an outdoor nature, involving exercise. However, in his opinion there should be indoor recreation as well, for it was bad for children to be on the streets at night, and to have undirected play. Sunday was a day set apart from the rest of the week, but it ought not to go unplanned — the activities of the Sabbath should be so arranged that the child would look forward with pleasure to the day. All this he set forth in his *Christian Nurture*. Henry Ward Beecher's view have already been discussed in connection with public health (p. 66). Channing also gave some thought to the subject. He didn't want people to derive their amusement from the misery of others,[80] while not objecting to literature that entertained, nevertheless he thought it ought to do more than merely amuse in order to justify itself[81] Channing wanted working men to have pleasures, of course! But he thought such pleasures would come through and be heightened by "self-culture". He thought Walter Scott's novels contributed much to the enjoyment of his readers, but a cultivated mind also found relaxation and joy in history, biography and other non-fictional writings. He hoped, too, for a type of amusement which would entertain, but which would be superior to the theatre of his own day.[82]

Henry Bellows took his stand for more play. Did he not address the theatrical people of New York on *The Relation of Public Amusements to Public Morality?* And this in a day when perhaps all Protestant Christians, save only the worldly Episcopalians, frowned upon the theatre. In this address he proposed "to show that amusement is not only a privilege but a duty, indispensable to health of body and mind, and essential even to the best development of religion itself." While he excepted such vices as drunkenness, lust and gambling, as not being amusements, he took a broad view. It was, he held, a necessity and not a luxury, and lack of it was "a calamity, and an injury to the sober and solid interests of society."[83]

Thus on the subject of benevolence, housing, public health and amusement, there were prominent New England clergymen and laity who had their say and made their contribution; in many ways it was remarkably sanely and scientifically done too. They did what they could according to their light, which was limited perhaps more by inadequate information than by the bounds of interest and ability to deal with these problems. Certainly it appears that they wanted to build a Christian social conscience to wrestle with these trying and serious matters.

CHAPTER VI

THE RACE QUESTION

It was not called the *race question* back there in the fore part of the nineteenth century, but it existed nevertheless.[1] Indians, as we well know, constituted the original inhabitants of America, and the advent of Europeans meant the introduction of a new type of living vastly different from that of the natives, soon provoking a clash of interests. Long before Jamestown (1607), white settlers suffered death at the hands of the aborigines,[2] and King Philip's War came in the last quarter of the 1600s.[3] Indian slavery proving futile, the labor supply being particularly short, colonists resorted to Negro slavery, every colony having had some slaves.[4] The coming of the black slave provided the second and major strand in our race problem. The third and minor one (in the period under discussion) was the bringing of the Chinese coolies to California shortly after gold was discovered in 1849.[5]

Very early American Christians recognized a sense of responsibility toward these less-privileged peoples. It will be remembered that the Pilgrims came to America (1) to establish their own religious and social order, and (2) to evangelize the natives.[6] About 26 years later John Eliot, of Massachusetts, became the first missionary to the Indians.[7] It is true that some leading clergymen of the colonial period owned slaves,[8] Eliot and Cotton Mather were not opposed to the institution, though both of them argued for humane treatment of the unfortunate creatures.[9] Dr. Samuel Hopkins, pastor of the First Congregational Church, Newburyport, Rhode Island, himself a slave-owner, came to view it as

70

a degrading system, and threw the weight of his influence against it. By 1770, he was denouncing the business of stealing, buying and keeping men in servitude, even at the expense of losing some members of wealth from his parish. Within the Revolutionary era, the Congregational clergy commonly came out against slavery.[10] Our period of present interest also witnessed the birth of New England recognition of underprivileged peoples in remote parts of the world. That interest, of course, had to do primarily with the salvation of their immortal souls. So in 1810 the American Board of Commissioners for Foreign Missions was formed — the work of the New England clergy.[11]

The extent to which the New England clergy and their followers were interested in the fate of the American Indian may be seen in the fact that "the Cherokee Mission [whose history was confined within the period under discussion] alone had cost $350,000, and 113 missionaries, men and women, ministers, teachers and artisans, had put their lives into it."[12] This was the work of the American Board which for many years undertook work among the natives.

On the day of the National Fast, in 1849, the Rev. Joseph G. Wilson asserted that Anglo-Saxons had robbed the Indian, [13] which was true enough. Ray Palmer, speaking at Bath, Maine, April 6, 1843, on *National Suffering the Result of Sins,* thought one of our country's outstanding evils was "our disregard of the great principles of justice and humanity."[14] He was referring specifically to our Indian affairs, where "Cupidity has trampled upon treaties, evaded positive engagements, and violated the rights of the feeble, whenever it has found occasion."[15] Thus he was convinced that "The red man has suffered and is suffering still through our injustice."[16] Yet there were those among the New England clergy whose interest in the natives' welfare was of a positive nature. The report of the Trustees of the Connecticut Missionary Society, for June, 1802, indicates that the Society had a Rev. Mr. Bacon who served as missionary to the Indians, that he was seeking an interpreter to aid him in his work among the Chippewas, who requested instruction in husbandry. Apparently Bacon was entirely willing to render this service and the Trustees approved.[17] The missionary referred to was David Bacon, father of Dr. Leonard Bacon.[18]

Among those who saw injustice done the Indian and pleaded his cause was the Rev. Jeremiah Porter, of New England stock, who was a representative of the American Home Missionary Society on the frontier. Porter's first assignment was at Sault Ste. Marie, where he lived in the home of the United States Indian Agent, Henry R. Schoolcraft, who was an ethnologist, and who later became a member of Congress. Schoolcraft's wife was an Indian, or a direct descendant of a famed Indian chief. No doubt in this atmosphere, the home missionary learned much conerning the Redskins, and it is not difficult to believe that the Indian Agent and the preacher often discussed matters which later appeared in the former's work: *Information Respecting the History, Conditions and Prospects of the Indian Tribes of the United States.*[19] At any rate Porter became a friend and advocate of the original inhabitants with whom his frontier life provided so many contacts. He attended revival meetings among the Indians, conducted by one of them, John Sandy, and spoke to them on invitation.[20]

Upon hearing that Black Hawk was making war on the whites, Porter asked: When will white men "treat the Indians as they should?" It was a judgment of God. (His information was incorrect regarding the success of the famous chieftain.) Porter believed the government of Upper Canada made better provisions for the native than did the

United States. There houses, mills and school-houses were erected, and schoolteachers were provided.[21] He chided the American Government for sending 10,000 soldiers against Black Hawk, the army killing about 200 starving Indians in three months of war. Probably 300 soldiers died of disease, and a million dollars was expended "to frighten poor natives." He thought one one hundredth of this amount used to support Christian missionaries among them might have averted this tragedy.[22] It is likely that Porter assisted Mrs. Schoolcraft in drafting the Constitution of the Algiac Society, which provided for constructive work among the Indians.[23]

Jeremiah Porter became the first settled Protestant clergyman in Chicago (1833). Here he cried out against the Government Treaty with the Winnebagoes, which was to force them to settle west of the Mississippi. He saw this thing continuing: "The mystery of iniquity does already work. When will the poor red man find a place to rest?"[24] How he deplored the avarice of white men who knew the Indian's weakness for whiskey and debauched him in order to relieve him of his money![25]

Indications are that missionaries of the American Board who served Indians were interested not only in their spiritual welfare, but were also interested in their intellectual advancement and physical well-being. The Reverend Cutting Marsh, famous missionary to the Indians, wanted a good mechanic to assist in the work.[26] A full-time teacher was required to instruct the children.[27] Marsh desired someone, too, who was expert in farming, to instruct the natives in the best arts of farming.[28] Perhaps the best evidence we have for believing that these New England clergymen who served as missionaries to the Indian were advocates of his social and physical welfare lies in the fact that their presence among the Indians was opposed by white exploiters.[29]

No doubt the interest of the New England clergy in the Negro question was tied up with the prevailing thought of the times, i. e., in the first period, at least, which ended about 1830, and which held a theoretical attitutde toward slavery and its abolition.[30] After 1830 there was a strong agitation for immediate abolition of slavery,[31] and innumerable sermons were preached from northern pulpits on the subject.[32] Various shades of opinion were to be found among the clergy. Leonard Bacon could hardly be described as an Abolitionist.[33] Bacon was identified, however, with two movements: (1) The American Colonization Society, founded in 1816, which had as its purpose the establishment of a republic in Africa for free Negroes from America and such slaves as might be liberated, and (2) the promotion of the well-being of the freedmen. He urged gradual emancipation,[34] and, in 1846, published *Slavery Discussed*, which, it is said, greatly influenced President Lincoln and finally led him to issue his Emancipation Proclamation.[35]

All the Beechers were against slavery,[36] and the Trustees of Lane Theological Seminary (Cincinnati) waited until President Lyman Beecher was in the East before forbidding the students to discuss the subject of abolition.[37] In the struggle for a free Kansas, Plymouth Church, Brooklyn, under the leadership of Henry Ward Beecher, undertook to supply every family going to the new state in the interests of freedom, with a Bible and a rifle,[38] the rifles came to be called *Beecher's Bibles*.[39] Every reader of American church history and of the slavery question knows the story of how he auctioned off slave girls to ensure their freedom.[40] But Beecher like Bacon, was not an Abolitionist. Lyman Abbott sums up his attitude thus:

> When an individual is engaged in wrong-doing, it is his duty immediately to cease wrong-doing; the doctrine of immediatism, applied by Dr. Beecher to the

individual is sound. When a community has become
pervaded by a social injustice which has been wrought
into its very structure, it is not always its duty,
by an immediate act of legislation, to destroy the
structure, in order that it may destroy the evil; the
duty of immediatism, applied to the community by
Mr. Garrison, was unsound.[41]

Beecher believed man-stealing was wrong, and that slavery
founded on it was evil; but he did not believe that immediate
abolition of the slave trade was the best and wisest method
of dealing with the problem "without preparation of either
slave or   society for a better industrial condition."[42] So
Abbott describes him not as an abolitionist, but as an anti-
slavery reformer.[43]

The influence of the New England parsonage was strong;
the minister's children often acquired the convictions of their
father. While Henry Ward Beecher had his way of dealing
with slavery, his sister, Harriet, wife of the Rev. Calvin
Stowe (who taught at Andover, Lane and Bowdoin), had
her unique but effective way of meeting it. She wrote her
Uncle Tom's Cabin, in which she cleverly portrayed slavery
both at its best and its worst, and she made her most loathe-
some character, the harsh overseer, a northern Yankee, and
not a Southerner at all. Her book made its way into homes
of every type and to the far corners of the earth. Indirectly
the fruit of the New England clergy, the book became one of
the outstanding factors in promoting civil strife and the
end of Negro bondage.

Theodore Parker was not an early abolitionist, but when
converted, he became an ardent one.[44]   At the Odeon, in
Boston, space could not accommodate the crowds who came
to hear him thunder against the evils of slavery; from
Massachusetts to the deep South he carried his message,

and he knew the importance of what he was doing — how thousands of persons in America and Europe would be influenced by what he said and did.[45] Like Beecher, he did much to aid the Kansas *free soilers;*[46] but unlike Beecher he went further, much further.[47] Parker sheltered fugitive slaves in his home, urged disobedience to civil laws, which he regarded as evil, and attacked public officials. His words were whips and scorpions which lashed judges, senators and even presidents. By the power of his eloquence he drove Judge Loring from the bench and compelled him to leave Boston. Public men felt constrained to explain to him their words and actions or their silence and inaction.[28] When indicted for illegal acts against the Government, he was so powerful, he so welcomed this opportunity, that the judge feared to proceed with the trial.[49]

No account of the New England socializer's relation to the race question, or slavery in particular, should be summarized without examining the statements of the scholarly and saintly Channing. He had much to say about the Negro and his enslavement. His basic assumption was that the discussion must begin with not what was profitable, but what was right, which was the supreme good, including all other goods. He proposed to deal with "great truths, inalienable rights, everlasting duties".[50] The issue was not being faced squarely. Either people felt so vehemently as to exclude clear thinking, or they simply declined to think about it at all. He did not like the concessions which were being made to slavery. Yet one was not emotionally and spiritually fitted to deal with this, or any of "the great interests of humanity" unless his heart was clean from anger, malice and uncharitableness.[51] This question of slavery was deserving of the best philosophical thought and Christian action.[52] "He who cannot see a brother, a child of God, a man possessing all the rights of humanity, under a skin darker than his own wants the vision of a Christian."[53] If we are unmoved by sympathy toward these millions in bonds, he said, we show ourselves not their superiors in Christian virtue.[54] Then Channing proceeded to indicate how (1) man, even a colored man, could not be rightly held as property, for if one man could be so held, all men could be held;[55] (2) man has certain rights, endowed by his Creator, and slavery infringes on those rights, such as an equivalent for his labor, or protection from impartial laws;[56] (3) the essential equality of men made it wrong;[57] (4) American society had come to regard the stealing of men from Africa as piracy; hence, if stealing men was evil so was holding them in bondage; the length of the evil did not diminish its character.[58] Channing proposed to show the evils in the system, itself, how it was morally debasing, intellectually sultifying, pernicious to home-life, conductive to cruelty, demoralizing to masters, and politically bad.[59] He had no sympathy with those, and there were many, who tried to prove from Scripture that slavery was approved of God.[60]

How to remove slavery became the important question. This was a matter, Channing thought, for the slave-holder himself to decide. He alone had sufficient knowledge concerning the slave, his habits, character and needs. Others might lay down general principles, but it was for the holders to work them out. Any dangers arising from Emancipation would be increased if it came by a "foreign hand".[61] Race riots in the twentieth century are the bitter fruit of a situation, which Channing foresaw as a possibility, as he viewed the matter a century ago:

Let him [the slave] feel that liberty has been wrung from an unwilling master, who would willingly replace the chain, and jealousy, vindictiveness, and hatred would spring up to blight the innocence and happiness of his new freedom, and to make it a peril to himself and all around him."[62]

But Channing had some suggestions as to what should
be done. Slaveholders must accept the principle that holding a man as property was wrong.[63] At present the slave
needed a guardian, not an owner. Slaves should be prepared
to support themselves.[64] Incentives should be offered them
for improving their lot. [65] Put the slave's family on a more
secure basis. [66] Stop buying and stealing slaves[67] All this
the slave-holder himself was to do without any outside com-
pulsion. Channing had no confidence in the colonization
scheme.[68]

Channing expressed his mind regarding abolition and
abolitionists. He deplored their persecution, because it was
in his very nature to defend the persecuted, no matter who
they were. That they were often accused of fomenting
trouble — falsely accused — he had no doubt. Abolitionists,
so far as he knew, were men of fine character and deeply
stirred by feelings of human compassion. Yet they were
wrong, and he could not close his eyes to this fact. All
enthusiasts, in which they were included, fell into the common error of taking a too narrow view of things. They made
exceptional cruelties toward the slave the prevailing condition. It was wrong to advocate immediate Emancipation.
While they offered some plausible explanations, most people
never read or heard the explanations; they were captured
by a phrase — so their objective was really "inconsistent
with the well-being of the slave and the order of the state."[69]
Nor could Channing bring himself to approve their system
of agitation — a criticism which he brought not only against
the abolitionists, but against the Age, when "Truth can
hardly be heard unless shouted by a crowd."[70] Such methods
relied on appeals to passion and not to reason; fruitful of
evil results.[71]

Frederick Frothingham, in 1857, declared: "We live in

days when men 'decree unrighteous decrees' . . ."[72] He was aware that this applied in various directions, but he thought slavery the most pressing of questions. Frothingham knew what lay behind the institution's perpetuity: "The appeal to the instinct of Property in the Northern mind finally settled the question."[73] Yet he foresaw the coming conflict. Advocates of slavery were more cunning than the opponents; the trade was without conscience. He urged his hearers to throw themselves "on the Eternal Law of God," and "brand the monster of iniquity," thus it would be possible to rid the nation of the evil. He saw such questions as Free Trade, Tariffs, and a National Bank retiring into the background, while the nations of the world would watch Americans fight out the issue of slavery.[74]

The Boston Fugitive Slave Case led Wm. H. Furness, of Philadelphia, to speak his mind. An entire sermon was devoted to it, in which he held that:

> Eternal Justice, that Truth which is from everlasting to everlasting, which no one questions, whatever else may be disputed, addresses us, and commands us to do for our wronged brother as we would have him do for us, were we in his place.[75]

Nothing less than this constituted the grand test of one's sincerity in his religion; evasion of it rendered religion worthless.[76]

Already allusion has been made to the practical measures taken in connection with the eradication of slavery: Beecher and Parker aiding the *free-soilers* to make Kansas a free state (p. 76). Oberlin, Ohio, became, with Boston, an important center of abolition sentiment and action. The First Parish Church and village (Oberlin) were an important station in the Underground Railway, which operated in behalf of runaway slaves, aiding them to escape to Canada.[77]

Other ways, too, the anti-slavery people, the more radical among them, had for making their ideas effective. The Rev. D. Nelson, of Quincy, Illinois, went over into Missouri to preach, but he denied the Sacrament of the Lord's Supper to slaveholders. Said he:

> I told my Christian brethren there, that I could not hand them the emblems of my Lord's body unless they washed away the blood which was dripping from their finger nails! Still they came, listened, and wept.[78]

He was no exception; in 1837 the New England Anti-slavery Society, in which many of the clergy were actively interested, adopted resolutions advocating excommunication of all slave-holders from the churches, and if a local church did not take sufficiently courageous action, the dissenting anti-slavery members were asked to form themselves into separate congregations.[79] This was actually done at Andover, Massachusetts, where the Free Christian Congregational Church was organized by the dissenters from South Church,[80] and the origin of the First Congregational Church, Chicago, came about in some such manner.[81]

Another means of making their ideas effective was tried — pressure was brought to bear upon the American Home Missionary Society to get the officials to deny any missionary aid to any clergyman whose congregation did not renounce slavery. Among those who thus sought to influence the Society was the Rev. H. Patrick, of Caledonia, Massachusetts, who wrote:

> I am aware that you have heretofore been in the habit of extending aid to ministers and churches, whom I cannot but view as being in the very spirit and practice of slavery . . . you must withhold aid from ministers and churches who are in the spirit

of *slave holding.*[82]

This failing, after a period of years, anti-slavery Congregationalists took matters into their own hands, and in 1846, or thereabouts, formed the American Missionary Association, in whose organization Oberlin College played a very important part, and which became properly anti-slavery.[83] The Society has had a long and distinguished career of usefulness, especially in these later years to the Negro, Indian and Mountain White.[84]

It was not simply a matter of freeing the Negro. True, it may be that most anti-slavery men thought so, but not all of them by any means. As early as 1835 Oberlin College opened its doors to Negroes on equal terms with the whites.[85] In 1839, a slave-schooner, *the Amistad,* providing a famous case in American diplomacy and International Law, was brought to New London, Connecticut, where Judge Story, after a considerable struggle, set the slaves aboard the vessel free. Congregational Lewis Tappan, a wealthy layman, solicited funds for their relief, and Connecticut Congregationalists cared for and educated them at Farmington. At last they were returned to Africa and the Mendi mission was begun.[86] Other efforts to aid the Negro were hampered, especially those in the South.[87]

No doubt other problems and issues were tied up with the Negro question, and it is also true that neither the New England clergy nor any other group saw slavery as a part of a much larger matter: the whole problem of race.[88] As early as 1813, Nathaniel Emmons, the New England divine, who had trained more than 100 young ministers in his home, was aware of sectionalism. He opposed the Louisiana Purchase, opposed the use of state militias and the creation of new states. Laws, he maintained, too often favored the South to the detriment of the North, and he advocated nullification.[89] In a later chapter we shall see how the New

England clergy denounced the War with Mexico. Undoubtedly one of the major reasons for this was that the ministers saw in the acquisition of more territory the extension of slavery.[90] Perhaps the Rev. W. H. Lord, of Montpelier, Vermont, came closer to the realization of the race problem than any of the others. At least he seems to be one who employed the term *race* in some such connection when he said:

> An exclusive affection for any race is no virtue, and is a sure mark of an unimproved heart. The jealousy, which, under the name of patriotism, regards with sinister emotions, the progress and influence of the foreign element, and cares for no portion of the human race but that to which it belongs, is an evidence of the folly and selfishness of an uncultivated mind.[91]

Extended interest in immigration arose comparatively late. True, several of the colonies had enacted laws governing the matter, and in 1798 Congress passed the Alien Bill.[92] But it was not until 1838 that a Congressional committee was named to investigate immigrant pauperism. The Government wavered in its policies from time to time.[93] But there were those among the New England clergy who discerned problems connected with the settlement of foreigners in our midst. Among them were the Rev. Messrs. A. D. Mayo, W. H. Lord and Orville Dewey. Mr. Lord noted the rising tide of irreligion, crime and pauperism chiefly in Boston and New York and other eastern centers of population, where the immigrant lived in large numbers. It was for the good of the country generally that the foreigner came; he tilled the fields and worked in the factory.[94] Lord thought if the immigrant were "kindly received and taught in his duties and responsibilities," given a period of probation and "publicly inducted into the high position of a citizen" with all its duties and privileges; if we permitted "patience, confidence and love" coupled with wisdom, to take "the place of bigotry, recrimination and exclusiveness", it wouldn't be long until "the foreign born will become assimilated and bring up their children as good patriots."[95] Mayo had come to believe that some people had degenerated to the level of professional defamers, but fortunately they were being rebuked, for the "best men are now deliberating over their obligations to those whose sins and misfortunes have placed them under the feet of society," and they were coming to see "a new evidence of the divine energy in human society . . ."[96] To meet the problems of immigration, Dewey proposed that the schools should impart the duties of citizenship to those who needed it.[97]

The story of foreign missions does not belong in this volume, yet in the matter of race relations it must be conceded that the missionaries have had a conspicuous part for the better. Wendell Willkie paid high tribute to these ambassadors of goodwill in a special article prepared for *Missionary Herald,* a Congregational paper, which was published in a 1943 number. Much of this work, as previously stated (p.   ) began in the period under discussion. In furtherance of better race relations, in part, Joseph Tuckerman began his outstanding career in social work. Tuckerman's ministry-at-large grew out of his interest, when in Chelsea, in men who sailed the seven seas, and whose ships brought them to Boston and other New England ports. Here he had ample time to see the sailors, how they were treated, and the kind of life they lived. So he thought of them, both for themselves and for the influence they would carry to such foreign places as those in far away China. He longed for clean, Christian sailors to represent America at its best, and thus he organized his Seamen's Society, which launched him on his career as a social worker.[98].

In the writing of this brief chapter, it was not to be expected than any significant contribution could be made to the history of the race problem or its solution. Yet it could not be excluded for excellent reasons. *First,* without it we should have had a distorted picture of the interest of the New England clergy in the socialization of Christianity. *Second,* out of slavery emerged certain principles which later called for application to other problems. For example: when Channing dealt with slavery he discovered that workers were entitled to a fair return for their services.[99] Furness learned about a law of social justice.[100] While Frederick Frothingham found that the poor and needy were unrighteously treated.[101] The clergy did much to call attention to the sad plight of our Indian affairs, they also raised our relations with Oriental peoples to a higher level while corrupt and selfish economic interests were trying to keep them on a low level. These ministers were thinking about the problem of immigration at an early date, constructively thinking about it.

CHAPTER VII

GOVERNMENT AND THE PENAL SYSTEM

The years under discussion witnessed things which tended to make intelligent men conscious of their government and its functions. America herself was passing through the experience of trying to make her own constitutional system work. What were the responsibilities and privileges of the Federal and State entities? Sectionalism, nullification, banking systems, war and peace, expansion and new states — all these and many more interesting problems involving a national debate are to be found written up in the history books. Add to this the fact that great struggles were on in Latin America and in parts of Europe to throw off the shackles of tyranny and to try democracy, and you have a fascinating era for thinking men.

Were all governments ordained of God, and therefore exempt from criticism? Was St. Paul adequately versed in political science and statecraft, was the apostle, who lived almost exclusively under Roman law and who took pride in his Roman citizenship, sufficiently unbiased to express an authentic opinion regarding the divine origin of all governments? Of course, the clergy did not explicitly deny Paul's doctrine, but their appeals to "the higher law" certainly afforded them opportunities to question the practices of those in charge of their Government.[1] It was only natural that the spiritual descendants of those New England clergy, who played so prominent a part in furthering American Independence,[2] should be interested in the work their fathers' hands had wrought in large part. Some of the representative ministers expressed their disappointment in the political situation, and in some instances felt they knew exactly where the responsibility lay. As early as 1813, Nathaniel Emmons, the New England theologian and trainer of young ministers, made up his mind not to preach a Thanksgiving sermon which extolled everything American. He had some unpleasant truths to share with his congregation. Oh, he granted that the first twelve years under the Federal Constitution were years in which "our rulers devised and pursued such measures as actually promoted our national interests, and respectability in the eyes of the world."[3] He was the Federalist speaking. Those good old days were gone, national policy had been changed, and a deplorable condition existed, he thought. The Louisiana Purchase, the use of state militias, the creation of new States, the enactment of laws governing commerce to the advantage of the South and the detriment of the North were some of the things which he characterized as so bad that he did not think the American people should submit to them. He wanted citizens to become articulate, and to resist.[4] Of course it may be properly pointed out that there may have been no great social ideal behind Emmons' statements, and that he was governed by sectional selfishness pure and simple. On the other hand, it may be equally true that he was conscious of no such selfishness, but actually believed he saw anti-social implications in the trends against which he inveighed. The significant point, however, is that he wanted no meek submission, but wished the American people to speak out.

Somewhat earlier than this (1812), Lyman Beecher exhorted his fellow-preachers that ministers should properly warn people of public guilt and danger. "They [the clergy] were watchmen, set upon the walls of Zion, to descry and announce the approach of danger."[5] He also knew that:

A free government is a government of laws made by

the people for the protection of life, reputation, and property. . . . Every man, conforming to the laws of his country, has a right to the peaceable enjoyment of life and all its immunities.[6]

The same laws, Beecher held, must apply to rich and poor. No man because he was rich and had an honorable reputation should be lightly sentenced or go free, when he committed some crime; his punishment should be as severe as that meted out to the poor who might be guilty of a similar offense.[7] As he looked out over his world, he became convinced that all governments needed some overhauling. Power concentrated in a few hands must be distributed among freemen. Society must be elevated; human energies must count in a well-ordered society. To accomplish this, the great mass of mankind must be educated and qualified for self-government, and submit themselves to delegated authority.[8]

Both the prominent and lesser luminaries of the New England pulpit expressed their views. Among the latter was Francis Convers, of Watertown, whose *Address Delivered on the Fourth of July,* 1828, contained his fears for the future of self-government, that it could not endure where an ignorant people were unable to appreciate its value or wield its power.[9] Convers did not believe that corruption in society would behave like a stagnant pool; rather it would

roll on, wave after wave, marking its progress by constantly higher encroachments, till it reaches and breaks over the eminences on which the directers (sic) of political power and political agencies stand.[10]

There was reason, of course, for the clergy to be concerned, for neither Theodore Parker nor Orville Dewey felt that a high state of morality and ethics prevailed in politics. Had not Andrew Jackson put into office men, some of whom were dishonest, many of whom were incompetent, and most of whom were inefficient? Was not this same system springing up in a number of states? Dewey, in New York City, would have known about that for it was there that the custom flourished, and it was a fellow-New Yorker, Marcy, who coined the phrase: " 'To the victors belong the spoils!' "[11] So the *spoils system* prevailed in national government. Parker saw the functioning of municipal government in Boston — another center of population — and he said: "In politics, it is not yet decided whether it is best to leave [it to] men [to] buy where they can cheapest, and sell where they can sell dearest, or to restrict that matter."[12] The Boston divine was sure, however, that "there is such a thing as an absolute right, a great law of God, which we are to keep, come what will."[13] So he and others of the clergy, of this era, were to appeal again and again to this higher law, in dealing with the issues of the day. Should a minister take an active part in politics? Parker had his answer ready: Of the clergy who avoided the issue, he said, "Such ministers ought to have nothing to do with anything, and soon will have what they ought."[14] Agreeing with Parker was Nathaniel H. Eggleston, out there in Wisconsin, who was somewhat scornful of those who "hold politics are too dirty for ministers to take part in them."[15] He resented the abuse heaped upon those of the clerics and churches which were somewhat active in politics.[16] T. W. Higginson, of Worcester, was likewise very positive. A bit startling was his proposition that: "We need more radicalism in our religion and more religion in our radicalism."[17] Religion, he thought, should preside over all "the reforms which are condensed revolutions," and, with no fear whatever concerning separation of Church and State, he plunged on: "In a right state of society; the theme of the pulpit during every summer should predict the matter of next winter's legislation."[18] More than likely, he did not mean merely to foretell what would take place, but rather that the Church should influence the trend in the direction which it believed to be right.

Dewey questioned the propriety of that attitude which held "all is fair when it comes to politics" — a feeling all too prevalent; persons who would not think of dishonesty in private life unhesitatingly passed and accepted bribes in public life. The first step toward the remedy lay in conscientious use of the ballot; it was the duty of all citizens to exercise their franchise in the highest interests of the whole; honest electors were indispensable.[19] Next there must be honest officials. Rigid loyalty to party and consistent opposition to the administration in power by legislators of the minority were alike deplorable, for under such circumstances, thought Dewey, "Parties, then, demand not honesty but service, of their votaries," and "Abuses become precedents, and precedents multiply abuses." In that condition, he feared, that: "Honorable citizenship is sunk in base partisanship," and "The national conscience is sold in the market. The national honor is all bowed down to the worship of interest."[20] So Dewey believed that corrupt government would continue till persons of wealth and learning assumed their just responsibilities.[21]

Horace Bushnell and Henry Ward Beecher, too, were interested in the political arena — not as office seekers, to be sure. Early in life Bushnell discussed such questions as the *Missouri Compromise,* whether a President should be elected under our present system or be chosen directly by the people, and whether a court, in its decisions, should regard the former character of a criminal.[22] It was impossible, in the opinion of Beecher, for anyone in a democracy to escape civic responsibility. There were times, he was sure, when articulate patriotism was only a cloak for something sinister. Beecher noted that it was often "made to

be an argument for all public wrong, and all private mean-
ness."[23] Beecher thought there were occasions when a man
might be safely unpatriotic (according to popular ideas)
and be right. No man was so unpatriotic, he held, as
Jesus of Nazareth, in Jerusalem, who put the needs of
men above laws and institutions.[24] He knew, too, that wise
and needed legislation must have public sentiment behind
it, for it is that sentiment behind good laws which protects
the city and frees the people of lawlessness and other evils.[25]
The Brooklyn preacher left this note of warning: "A State
in which the citizen is the pabulum of the state, will soon
have nothing left to feed on,"[26] a warning, we of the 1940s
are seeing fulfilled before our very eyes.

Perhaps we are indebted most to Channing for the
Christian man's philosophy of government. Both his
essay on "The Union," and his "Duties of the Citizens in
Times of Trial or Danger," contain significant passages.
The function of all governments, he held, was primarily
negative, and this was especially true of the Federal
Government, which held the States together. Its greatest
duty was to avert evil. This was nothing against government, since "The highest political good, liberty, is negative."[27] "The great good of the Union we may express almost in a word. It preserves us from wasting and destroying one another."[28] If the Central Government were to fail,
if the States were broken up into so many small nations
they "would be arrayed against one another in perpetual,
merciless, and ruinous war." The National Government
was our defense against foreign powers. So great was his
appreciation of this fact, that he asked for nothing more
from the General Government than to hold the States
together, and "to establish among the different States relations of friendship and peace."[29] The disintegration of
the Union would produce "fierce and implacable enmi-

ties."[30] A common language, so advantageous to the Union, in the event that the Union failed, would produce untold harm.[31] If division should come, the individual States would form stronger bonds with foreign powers than with one another. Europe would step in, and establish its influence over us. Belligerents in the Old World would seek to enlist our individual States in their quarrels. In the event that the States should withdraw from the Union, there would be more party politics within those States than under the federal system.[32] This party-spirit, he deplored, as an evil thing. It was the outstanding enemy of patriotism.[33]

Channing had reason to speak and write as he did. *Nullification* had been used first by Kentucky, in 1798, to express views on the trend toward centralization in government.[34] South Carolina was debating it in the quadrennium just preceding his essay on "The Union,"[35] which was in the nature of a reply to John Quincy Adams, who accused his own State of trying to dissolve the Union.[36]

Did Channing have any suggestions as to how the Union could be preserved to serve its purpose well? He did, and he was quite willing to share his ideas. The greatest simplicity should characterize the Government. Laws should be plainly worded and based on those principles understood by the people. This rule should be applied to all republican forms of government. Those laws should be comparatively few.[37] Apparently he and Thomas Jefferson saw eye to eye in this matter of simplicity in government. In his first inaugural address, the President had said that his administration would offer "a wise and frugal government, which shall restrain men from injuring one another, and shall leave them otherwise free to regulate their own pursuits of industry and improvement. . . ."[38] There must be a free press, Channing held, whose task it would be to keep the people informed on all measures to be brought before them for decision.[39] He thought the sin of all governments was that "they intermeddle injuriously with human affairs, and obstruct the processes of nature by excessive regulation."[40] The Boston clergyman's reasoning had a strangely familiar ring in the recent political campaign. Our foreign and domestic policies should not be shrouded in mystery — those policies "should be perspicuous and founded on obvious reasons. . . ."[41] Legislators should be sensitive to their responsibility to offer legislation marked by "all possible simplicity, and to abstain from measures which, by their complication, obscurity, and uncertainty must distract the public mind, and throw it into agitation and angry controversy."[42] The National Government, he called the *General Government,* and that was what he wanted it to be. Channing deplored sectionalism. Federal laws should not be enacted to further the special interests at the expense of the whole. Congress, he thought, was being more and more overwhelmed by a multiplicity of things, thus preventing it from dealing efficiently with those matters rightly within its sphere. Already he heard the angry complaints against the inefficiency and bungling of Congress, which would increase until the legislative branch confined itself to its legitimate realm of action.[43]

Channing did not approve of the Government's restrictive attitude in connection with business — he thought it "bode no good for the Union,"[44] So he was against the tariff, which was restrictive, which was fruitful of discord, and which was enacted "to protect certain branches of domestic industry."[45] Channing believed that people would much more readily accept disadvantages "imposed by nature" than "those which are brought on them by legislation."[46] This whole idea of protection was repugnant to him, and he believed to the American people. It was deceptive. It was not in keeping with the American tradition. "To this country, above all others, belongs, as its primary duty and interest the support of liberal principles."[47] Tariffs savored of provincialism.

> As citizens of the world, we grieve that this country should help to prolong prejudices which even monarchy is outgrowing. . . . As patriots, we grieve that a precedent has been afforded for a kind of legislation which, if persisted in, will almost certainly loosen, and may rupture, the Union.[48]

The gentlemanly Channing could on occasion become satirical. "The principle excellences of the late tariff is, that it is so constructed as to please no one. . . ."[49] No tariff was impartial. It resulted from "selfish combinations of private and public men".[50] If he could have closed every customs house in the Union, he would have done it gladly. Apparently it was, under existing circumstances, a necessary evil, providing revenue for the Government; but it should not be allowed to do more than furnish inome. Free trade was essential to a world civilization; fetters between nations must be broken. But even this matter of national income troubled him. It was a form of indirect taxation, which he abhorred. A free people "ought to know what they pay for freedom, and to pay it joyfully. . . ." Citizens "should as truly scorn to be cheated into the support of their government as into the support of their children."[51] Nor should any government have an overflowing treasury, for "An overflowing treasury will always be corrupting to the governors and the governed."[52]

Nor was Channing impressed favorably with public works programs sponsored and paid for by the Federal Government, that is, such as were clearly local in character. Those benefiting the general or national welfare might be acceptable.

But let Congress propose narrow, local improvements, and we need no prophet to foretell the endless and ever-multiplying intrigues, the selfish combinations, the jealousies, and discontents which will follow by a necessity as sure as the laws of nature,[53]

Government subsidies for canals, railroads, etc., did not appeal to him. The Federal Government itself did more than all these to promote intercourse. If Congress would only follow a course destined to hold the people together in peace and unity, he felt that:

the spirit of the people will not slumber. It will pour itself forth through our State Governments, through corporations, and through individual enterprise; and who that observes what it has already done can set the limits to its efficiency?"[54]

Channing was of the opinion that the danger lay in over-action on the part of the Government, from selfishness and impatience, and from too rapid growth. "A calm, sober, steady government is what we chiefly need."[55] If the present-day politicians knew their Channing, how some of them would quote him: "May it [the Federal Government] be kept from the hands of theorists and speculators!"[56]

The postal system, Channing held, was a tremendous boon to national unity, one which was not fully appreciated and used by the people. It ought not to yield income to the Government, if it paid its own way, that was enough. An independent judiciary with dignity, commanding the respect of all, was another asset to unity. Congress and people alike should feel that the Courts were primarily concerned with the preservation of the Union. Courts should offer aggrieved persons the lawful opportunity to resist what they regarded as an invasion of their constitutional rights. From the judiciary, Channing passed to the executive department of the

Government. He did not like presidential elections as they were being conducted. "A remedy must be found, or the country will be thrown into perpetual convulsions, and split into factions devoted each to a chief."[57] He feared too much waste "in struggles for a few leaders, who, by their prominence, will become dearer to a people than their institutions. . . ."[58] There was a danger of slavery in contending for a favorite candidate. "A people should understand its own greatness and dignity too well to attach much importance to any individual."[59] Of course a free society needed its presiding officer, but no man was indispensable; what it needed was a "President, not to be its master, but to express and execute its own will."[60] So:

> The only law of a free pople is the will of the majority, or public sentiment; and to collect, embody, utter, and execute this, is the great end of its civil institutions. Self--government is its great attribute, its supreme distinction, and this gives to office in a free state an entirely different character from what it possesses in despotic countries.[61]

Channing was willing to accord the Presidency its significant place. Important duties were laid upon the President, "but not such functions as can be discharged only by one or two individuals in the country, not such as ought to make him an object of idolatry or dread. . . ."[62]

Presidents were not always the most important figures in national life. He was ready to cite specific persons who, he did not think, were outstanding as national executives: Mr. Monroe and Mr. Adams. "They gave no spring to the public mind."[63] Congress had been guilty, he charged, of spending more time in advancing the cause of rival candidates than it had in the performance of its national duties. Monarchy was still the most widely functioning form of government in his day, so Channing's remark was pertinent:

We shall do well to remember that a republic, broken
into parties which have the chief magistracy for their
aim, and thrown into perpetual agitation by the rival-
ry of popular leaders, is lending a mournful testimony
to the reasonings of monarchists, and accelerating the
fulfillment of their sinister forebodings.[64]

Channing paid his respects to the Federalists. No purer
party was ever in power. To be sure it contained certain
weak men, and certain bad ones. In times of prosperity it
brought self-seeking men to its ranks. Nevertheless, it was
a great party. Yet he could not give them an entirely clean
bill of health. They were guilty of crime, "they were criminal
in the despondence to which they yielded. . . ."[65] They
lacked faith in our system, they were without that hope
which "hopes against hope" and which is so necessary to
inspire freedom. This was the Federalists' sin, for this they
paid the penalty of being driven from office.[66] The opposition, too, had its weaknesses. Virginia's alien and sedition
laws, Georgia's dealings with the Indians were cited as ex-
amples. Partisan-minded men would not have liked Channing's stand. But what of it? Had not the time come when
slavish loyalty to party politics should end? Whoever en-
courages and diffuses the broader way "will deserve a place
among the most faithful friends of freedom."[67]

Eloquent in his support of the Federal Government,
Channing could also advocate another course on occasion,
and the War of 1812 provided that occasion. Governments
existed, he held, for the sole purpose of protecting the
governed, to promote their peace and welfare. When governments failed in this essential duty, it not only became
legitimate, but a duty, to offer opposition. He maintained:

So far is an existing government from being clothed
with an inviolable sanctity, that the citizen, in particular circumstances acquires the right, not only of

remonstrating, but of employing force for its destruction. This right accrues to him when a government wantonly disregards the end of social union. . . .[68]

Closely associated with government was the penal system for dealing with crime. On this subject not a few of the clergy expressed their views. Opinions were various, ranging from mild to severe treatment for the punishment of criminals. Dr. E. N. Kirk (was it because he lived in Albany, the capital of New York State, that he took his stand?) held to the lawfulness of capital punishment for murder. It was Scriptural, and he believed Jesus sanctioned it.[69] Samuel J. May, a leading Unitarian divine, a prime mover in the New England Non-Resistance Society, was against it — in fact the Society had as one of its cardinal tenets, the principle that it was wrong, both for individuals and for the State, to take a human life.[70] William Furness, of Philadelphia, appears to have gone even further than May, for he wrote: "The doctrine of entire abstinence from the use of force seems to me to be written in the very front of Christianity."[71] Timothy Stow, E. N. Chapin, Theodore Parker, all found something wrong with the penal system. Stow laid responsibility for crime at the very doors of political parties and governments, which oppressed or neglected the poor, which kept men captive when they ought to have been free, and which practiced evil means to secure desired ends.[72] Chapin regretted that society acted on the principle of retaliation, which was not sensible. Men ought not to be sent to prison as payment for wrong-doing, and then after a number of years be turned loose to commit more crime. He did not think the State had finished its work, when it had "inflicted pain, or loss, or restraint upon the criminal." That was no way to accomplish public security. There was only one intelligent reason for incarcerating persons guilty of crime, that was to reform them. Successful penal systems must culminate in a therapeutic service. So he had no sympathy for the system which sentenced men for a term of years, according to the nature of the crime. They should be kept so long as it was necessary to effect a cure and no longer. Society, in dealing with the criminal, was always to remember that he was still a man.[73]

As usual, we find Theodore Parker expressing himself in vigorous terms. One could always depend on Parker to take a prominent part in almost any reform. It was his yearning to see Christianity fully socialized.[74] So we note that as a student in Harvard Divinity School he was doing what John Wesley and his seventeenth century associates did while students at Oxford — visited those in prison. Parker went over to Charlestown prison to preach, but also to watch. In time he came not only to observe what he saw in his path, but he made his path to take him where he could make wider observations. Statistics regarding crime, he collated from his own State, from New York, and from Britain. The fault, he concluded, lay not only in the erring individual, but likewise with Society, and its two outstanding institutions: Church and State.[75]

No wonder that the smug Bostonese of his day, they who believed their city to be the Athens of America, the Hub of the Universe, they who thought Beacon Hill contained God's elect, were alarmed at this Parker. Within the very shadow of Old South, King's Chapel, and State House, he was saying:

> Every jail is a monument, on which is writ in letters of iron that we are still heathen, and the gallows black and hideous, the embodiment of death, the last argument a 'Christian' state offers the poor wretches it trained up to be criminals, stand there, a sign of our infamy. . . .[76]

So Parker attended the "Anti-Capital Punishment Convention," which he regarded simply as evidence of the new age. He was dubious of the penal system as a deterrent to crime and as a reforming agent; when Westover Reform School burned, he shed no tears over it. A school which educated youth in evil ways could not help but graduate criminals.[77] We are able to imagine the vehemence with which he cried: "Down must fall the gallows — type of a malignant God. . . ."[78] Parker wanted righteousness to visit the dungeon. So far as he was concerned, the third degree was definitely *out;* jails were not to be torture chambers, but civil hospitals to heal sick men — a sick man, that was what a criminal was. Crime, he thought, must be so dealt with that correction would be a means of blessing. To get rid of crime, society must free itself from drunkenness; America must forge her sharpest weapons to strike at "that beast with seven ghastly heads, and seventy times as many ampletined horns all red with murder; drunkenness must die."[79] In Parker's mind the twin evil of drink was poverty. In the struggle against crime, if Society were to win the battle, pauperism, too, "must lay off its rags."[80] To win the contest, it was not only necessary to reform our prison systems, but to change those habits and customs which produced criminals.

Again we are indebted to Channing for thinking this thing out. He did not believe the highest function of Government was to "make roads, grant charters, originate improvements, but to prevent or repress crimes against individual rights and the social order."[81] It was for this purpose that penal codes were adopted, prisons built and punishments inflicted.[82] Yet he thought that: "Arbitrary and oppressive laws invite offence."[83] The wisest legislation never went contrary to, but was somehow tied up with men's conscience. He felt that in actual practice our judicial system corrupted the moral sense of the community, and that a reform was overdue.[84] So Channing discussed the penal code. Like Lyman Beecher, he saw the law manipulated in favor of the rich and powerful and to the disadvantage of the poor.[85] It had been said, and he thought it true, that "the amount of property taken by theft and forgery is small compared with that taken by dishonest insolvency."[86] The thief guilty of the lesser crime went to prison, the bankrupt free.[87] Men sent to jails for debt — honest debtors, of course — shocked him; it was stark barbarism to allow "a creditor to play the tyrant over an innocent man. . . ."[88] The rich man who defrauded was as much a criminal as the poor who stole; the wealthy who drank to excess were certainly worse than the poor, who were driven to it by want; and the young man who seduced a girl was more deserving of punishment than the girl who was lured into prostitution.[89]

Prevention of crime challenged Channing. Laws should be simple and few, and the justice and humanity of them apparent to all. Wise punishment should aim at reform. Severe penalties did not decrease, but actually increased crime. Unfortunately our penal system until recent times had tended to harden the criminal in his resolve to thwart the law; first offenders were placed with old veterans. Humanity was glad to note some improvement throughout the country. "To remove the convict from bad influences is an essential step to his moral redemption."[90] But it was not enough. Individual Christians ought to sponsor individual prisoners, become sincere friends to encourage and help them —— a policy actually tried by the Rev. H. D. Southard, a Cleveland Methodist Minister, about the time of the first World War, with happy results. This was good Christianity, which never gave up the hope of redeeming men. Mercy was to temper legislation.[91] Channing had other ideas, too, about the prevention of crime. Like Parker, he believed drink to be a most important contributor to criminal behavior. Channing objected to efforts to annul existing laws aimed at suppressing the use of intoxicants. He saw "poor-houses, work-houses, jails and penitentiaries . . . tenanted in a great degree by those whose first and chief impulse to crime came from the distillery and dram-shop,"[92] murder and theft infrequently occurred as a result of drinking. Was not the Government bound to do something to prevent this by legislation, instead of using punishment, which was only inferior to the crime itself.[93] Do something about poverty, change the environment, stimulate an interest in self-culture, and you will have gone a long way in crime prevention.[94]

Somebody must put forth practical efforts to test the theories of the social philosopher. Parker and Channing, although they were more than social philosophers, were primarily that in relation to penology. The man who took it upon himself to work it out was Dr. Joseph Tuckerman. Of the thirty-nine social agencies in Boston in his day, a number of them were interested directly or indirectly in penology.[95] So it was not surprising that this friend of man should have given his talents and time freely in some attempt to solve the problem. Entries in his Journal indicate that within a short space of time he revealed his interest by frequent visits to penal institutions and courts. On November 5, 1826, he talked with female inmates at the House of Correction, on reasons for prayer; tactfully enough he did not tell them why *they* should pray, but why *we* should do so. Before the end of the month, he spoke to the men in the same institution. Before the middle of the next month, he was again at the House of Correction — this time to examine the condition of the insane, who were housed there. Tuckerman proposed to write the Governor, in an effort to secure legislation, to provide for other accommodations than prison cells for these unfortunates. On the 10th of January he was at Leverett St. Prison, to see some prisoners, and on the

27th he went to the House of Industry, and also stopped at the School for Juvenile Delinquents. In order to get some boys into the latter institution, he went to the Police Court on February 10th.[96] In 1827, after several efforts in their behalf, Tuckerman rejoiced to see the infamous Massachusetts law, which obligated the judiciary to send unindicted and unconvicted mental incompetents to jail, changed.[97]

If the reader is not too greatly impressed with Tuckerman's efforts and achievements, just let him remember that the Unitarians of Boston generously turned over to him all the poor and needy of the city, as well as other unfortunates, for his ministrations. His work with those in penal institutions constituted only a small part of his city-wide parish of the underprivileged. This fact stands out, many of the New England clergy of the era under discussion were interested, and they spent their efforts in behalf of better government, including a reform of prison conditions.

CHAPTER VIII

AGRICULTURE AND INDUSTRY

The purpose of this chapter is not to give a detailed account of problems associated with agriculture and industry. Nor is it likely that the ideas of the New England clergy will be accepted, in entirety, as the solution for them. The writer does hope, however, to give a faithful account of what he has found among the writings of the ministers, which pertain to agriculture, industry and economics.

As was previously stated (p. 61), America, in the period under discussion, was overwhelmingly a rural nation — a major part of our population living on farms. Modes of transportation were still limited, urban centers comparatively small and few. People in the country areas were thrown pretty largely on their own resources, not only for food and clothing, but for amusements as well. Again and again it has been said that the American farmer was and is an individualist. So undoubtedly agricultural problems were, to a considerable extent, regarded as personal matters. Growth of cities in the East and wars abroad modified the picture. Growing cities and European lands came more and more to depend on the agrarian West and South for food and cotton.[1] Affairs of the farmer became a national and even an international question. But interest in the problems of agriculture developed slowly. It was not until 1857 that there was introduced into Congress a measure for proposing the establishing of state agricultural schools, or even encouraging their establishment. Not until 1862 was such a law enacted.[2] There was considerable experimentation with the invention of new farming implements, but for various reasons no sudden or widespread use of such new machinery came to pass.[3]

Our public domain was extensive, pioneers moved in great numbers to far frontiers, and took up homestead claims.[4] But there is no indication that churches and religious leaders in the East were indifferent. On the contrary, much was done by eastern clergymen and their congregations to encourage their friends and relatives in the West. In 1826, the American Home Missionary Society was organized — an institution sponsored especially by Congregationalists and Presbyterians — to operate on a national scale. In its first year, this society contributed $18,140.00 to support 169 missionaries,[5] perhaps a majority of whom went to agricultural regions. Such organizations as the United Domestic Missionary Society and the Connecticut Home Missionary Society had rendered similar service, on a more restricted scale, previous to the founding of the national body. Comparatively little, however, has thus far been brought to light regarding the interest of the New England Clergy in specific farm problems. That little does contain some significant ideas. Paucity of material may possibly be due to the fact that the urban preacher gets into print much more readily than does his rural colleague; and being published his messages are more apt to be preserved and housed where the historian and research student find them more easily. Thus there may have been more interest displayed than we are aware of. Men whose messages we have studied were largely city pastors, concerned with issues near at hand. Possibly, too, land hungry Americans had alienated the sympathies of an anti-slavery eastern clergy, for in writing to Henry Clay, Channing protested the desire for more territory: "It is full time that we should" restrain ourselves. "Possessed of a domain vast enough for the growth of ages," he thought it was right that we should stop trying to get more.[6] Not that Channing himself was disinterested in the farmer and his needs — far from it, as we shall have occasion to see! Certainly when Nathaniel Emmons, back in 1813, denounced the tariff, Louisiana Purchase, etc., New England economy must have had much to do with his attack.[7]

Two members of the clergy took, perhaps, a somewhat optimistic view of the farmer's lot, although both of them placed high value upon him and his services. J. S. Buckminster, of Brattle Church (Unitarian), Boston, did not foresee the day of great American cities, consuming everything. He believed in an agrarian society and would have opposed the idea of reducing the farmer to a peasant status. But of this latter he had no fears whatsoever.[8] Henry Ward Beecher, the city minister, glorified the soil and the life of the farmer. Land, said he, from the beginning of time, had been the mother and nurse of healthy men. Cities themselves would degenerate if they were not saved by the influx of rural people. No other occupation offered so much independence as the life of the farmer, and any nation which had a large proportion of its population on the farms would not lack for good citizens.[9]

The Rev. Henry B. Pearson, at the First Congregational Church, of Harvard, Worcester County, Massachusetts, on the day of the Annual Fast, April 6, 1846, attempted to make the farmer conscious of his lot. Perhaps, in our modern day, by those who opposed his views, he would have been labelled a *rabble rouser*, or something of the sort. At any rate he spoke to them directly: "You, the producers, the farmers. . . ." He told them that it was they who raised the food, it was they, with the co-operation of laborers in factories, who made life possible for "the legislators, the lawyers, the politicians, the priests, the doctors, and every man and woman who is not a producer. . . ."[10] Pearson thought the farmer was the most important man in the country. Yet look at the statute books! Were there any laws written there to protect the farmers? He found none for their benefit, nor for factory hands. But tariffs protected the manufacturer. There were corporation laws enacted by the Federal Government to "infuse life into that soulless monster, called a Corporation, which coins gold out of the poor man's sweat."[11]

It was not likely that Horace Bushnell, had he known about Pearson's views, would have approved them. Bushnell feared agrarian laws. But, we are told, it was not because of any lack of interest in or love for farming.[12] Apparently a considerable number of the farmers believed in him or thought he had something of importance to say to them, for they invited him to address them at the Hartford County Agricultural Society in October 1846. At that time he made a strong plea for scientific farming, and for better social life among the farmers.[13] He feared for the future of the small farmer, the "support and comfort of their families. . . ."[14] Bushnell noted how, in Vermont, a few persons were buying up tract after tract and converting small farms which had failed into pasture lands. The rate of increase in population in Vermont, between 1830 and 1840, was smaller than at any other time since 1790. Other New England states, except for their cities, were not faring any better than Vermont in those days of the great westward migrations. So he feared that a small number of great landholders would make it a practice to come in, to buy up impoverished farms. Later great estates would be improved and cultivated. Sons of the farmers in Bushnell's generation would become peasants and serfs under wealthy landlords. To counteract this evil tendency, Bushnell advocated two remedies: He had great faith in scientific methods of farming, employed by small farmers. Put text-books on agriculture into the schools, where these superior methods could be learned. Moreover, the farm must be made more attractive, if youth and others were not to be lured away. There must be better housing. Neat, comfortable, nice looking houses would keep people, accustomed to the land, close to the soil.[15]

William Ellery Channing and Leonard Bacon, too, thought on these things. The latter, like Bushnell, was invited to address an agricultural society — in this case it was the New Haven County Agricultural Society, at its annual fair, September 27, 1848. Bacon was concerned with the proper fertilization of the soil. Future generations would pay a heavy price, if short-sighted farmers of his day continued to neglect to feed the ground. He also foresaw a day when the city's waste materials could and would be used to fertilize the farm.[16] In this he has been quite right. Fertilizers have been and are being produced from the waste materials gathered from butcher shops, grocery stores, restaurants, and even homes through garbage collection maintained by municipal governments.

The cityward trend of population worried Channing. Crowding the cities with rural people led to demoralization and the neglect of farming.[17] See to it that good taste was developed in the farmer. A little imagination on the part of country-dwellers could render grounds and cottage immensely more attractive. People would want to remain on the farm, then. He wanted every farmer to study and know chemistry. This would enable him to understand the needs of the soil, the needs of the different kinds of produce, and what kind of fertilizers would be essential to the right combinations, etc., for the growth of crops.[18]

Lyman Beecher saw possession and distribution of the land as a great international problem. Most of mankind who tilled the soil did so as "slaves or tenants." Large tracts were concentrated in few hands: kings, military leaders,

nobles and others. They in turn rented to landlords, who
sublet acreage to still others, who again subdivided it among

> the majority, who paid the rent . . . sustained, in the
> sweat of their brow, not only their own families, but
> three or four orders of society above them . . . and
> have been themselves crushed beneath the weight
> . . .[19]

Many of them "lived on the borders of starvation."[20] This
monopoly "of the soil must be abolished," he held. It was
sending people to the cities, to manufacturing, to wear
themselves out in industry, to be ignorant, hopeless and
poor.[21] Persons who worked the soil had a right to own it.
Such ownership of the land would mean their freedom, from
which would spring commerce, science, arts, liberty and independence.[22]

But it rested with still another clergyman to assist the
farmer in more practical ways. The Rev. Edward Hitchcock,
pastor of the Congregational Church at Conway, Massachusetts, about 1825, became interested in the study of
chemistry and geology. In time he became the president of
Amherst College, where his influence, no doubt, increased,
and his voice was heard afar. At any rate, in 1850, the
State of Massachusetts selected him to visit Europe in order
to examine the work of the agricultural schools over there.[23]
Unfortunately the American farmer had to wait for seventeen more years to pass, before the State Agricultural College
of Massachusetts — the first in the United States — became
a reality.[24]

At the same time that some of the New England clergy were indicating their awareness of agricultural problems,
they and others of their number were also thinking and
speaking about industry and the lot of the workers. This
interest was timely, for as Professor H. J. Carman has
pointed out, the laboring classes, before the Civil War, were

ignorant, politically weak, and the victims of exploitation on the part of speculators, liquor interests, employers and gamblers. Debtors' prisons continued to exist, and, in many, if not in most respects, their lot was pitiable.[25]

Now it was one thing to ask for philanthropy to ameliorate the awful sufferings of poverty-stricken, submerged elements in society. It was quite another thing to examine the causes, to find industrial and economic conditions responsible for the sad plight of the underprivileged, and to attack the system. It must have required tremendous courage on the part of prominent clergymen to place before their congregations, consisting of persons who became prosperous under the existing order, their candid views concerning such abuses as unhealthful working conditions and inadequate wages. Yet these ministers spoke in no unmistakable terms, as we shall see.

In *A Review of the Year,* a sermon delivered in Concert Hall, Cleveland, December 31, 1854, the Rev. A. D. Mayo, a clergyman of that city, spoke his mind. He was entirely fair. No one was blameless for "disasters in commerce". Mayo rebuked the farmer for neglecting his work, for short-sightedness and for his reluctance to use new means and machines to help his work. Mechanics too often lived beyond their means and thus destroyed sympathy for better pay, especially when they did inferior work. He went after the merchants guilty of using high pressure methods to get people to buy beyond their ability to meet obligations. The money-changer who grew rich from the wants of others; the people who used their money for luxuries instead of the common good, all came in for their share of criticism. Not even the Church escaped: "And even the church, that should be a pattern of the noble economy which saves from outward display to bestow for human comfort and culture, catches the general fever, and builds costly chapels for the wealthy few, from whose towers we may overlook more paupers than their walls could hold."[26]

The Rev. H. A. Boardman, D. D., of Philadelphia, took Thanksgiving Day, 1853, on which to speak of *The Low Value Set upon Human Life in the United States.* He excoriated the product of the industrial system — the general result. "Men were allowed to erect buildings which may tumble down of their own frailty, and bury a crowd of inmates beneath their ruins."[27] Unseaworthy ships were so frequently launched that it was no news to hear they had not survived a storm, it was a miracle when they did reach port safely. Railroads were operated with reckless abandon, in which "Conductors and engineers whirl their crowded trains into other trains, down precipices, and into drawbridges. . . ."[28] For these conditions he held the superintendents and boards of directors responsible, accusing them of conducting affairs so as to induce accidents, all because they knew they would escape any penalties. There was a reason for this deplorable state of things, and he knew the reason. It consisted in a "feeling business is of more importance than life, and speed is better than safety."[29] Boardman was aware that selfishness and greed were at the bottom of it; the country had gone insane over the love of money. Hence the flimsily built railroads, with single sets of tracks on the busiest routes, "fragile cars, incompetent conductors and engineers, unfaithful and overworked attendants, no adequate signals, no systematic inspection of machinery," etc.[30] This love of money was responsible for "steamboats like eggshells, worthless boilers, cabins constructed with a single outlet, by a narrow spiral staircase, for two or three hundred passengers, moveable lamps and candles. . . ."[31]

From his own pulpit, the Rev. Thomas Starr King, pastor of Unitarian Hollis St. Church, Boston, delivered two addresses, September 21, 1851. Evidently a special showplace had been erected to commemorate an important day in railway history, for his subject was *The Railroad Jubilee,* and he "imagined another crystal palace placed near the great receptacle of the world's labor, and filled with typical selections from the *laborers* that produced those things."[32] He thought it would furnish *some* commentary "upon our religion and the love of our neighbor" to go from the one building to the other, where one could also see

the squalor, the degradation, the miserable poverty, the unprotected disease, the carelessness of any refinement, the worn and distorted frames, half-fed and scantily clothed, the lack of glee in childhood, the absence of home in maternal eyes, the feeble gleams of the noble traits of our humanity in the faces of all, men, women and children; to whose steady toil from dawn till dark, — with scarce a respite through the years, till the drained and crippled body drops useless into the grave,—those triumphs of skill are due![33]

King accused the consuming public of a greater love for coal at five dollars per ton than for the miner's "manhood and domestic comfort, if they add another shilling to its price. . . ."[34] People demanded inexpensive garments, even though "the children of the widow-seamstress cry for food".[35] He scorned the desire for perfect pins, which converted 50,000 men into mere automatons, mere appendages to the machines which they operated; and he denounced the desire for cheap goods, which required that children should heed the call of the factory-bell, and not the school-bell. This preacher had no use for elegant laces at reasonable prices, which forced some woman "to stitch her honor and the peace of her life into the tender mesh, to prolong her existence in a hostile and desolate world."[36]

Orville Dewey, there in growing New York City, ob-

served what King saw in Boston, that working men came to
be regarded as machines "to produce and manufacture comforts and luxuries for those who can buy them."[37] So he resented the term *operatives* applied to *men* and *women* who
tended the machinery for production. This New York divine objected to the snobbish attitude of the few toward the
many, simply because the latter were laborers.[38] Dewey
thought: "The game which men were playing was too rapid,
and the stakes too large, to admit of the calm discriminations
of conscience, and the reasonable contemplation of moral
ends."[39] Wealth itself came to be regarded as an end, the
sooner attained the better. But a man could as surely and
completely sacrifice his integrity and soul in a place of business as in a gambling house or a brothel.[40] He looked at the
dangers of competition in business and over-expansion of
credit. Concentration of wealth in a comparatively few
hands bothered him: "Can it be right, that ten [men] should
grow to immense wealth, and that nine hundred and ninety
should for ever be poor?"[41] So Dewey came to plead the
cause of the working classes. He vigorously denied that
poverty was a virtue to the poor, and that money would
somehow increase their vices. In fact it was just the other
way around: "Let me tell you, that poverty is the parent of
improvidence and of crime."[42] Perhaps it was true that
those "who have been brought up in that school" would
temporarily "abuse their increased means."[43] But eventually
it could not be true. Give men something to hope for, some
means of improving their lot, some part "in the order and
welfare of society; and they will become less wasteful, less
reckless and vicious."[44] Like James Truslow Adams, who
is admittedly a reliable historian,[45] he contended that no
man builds a fortune by his own labors and his own property
alone, but that he uses the labors and property of others.
Those who cheated and went into bankruptcy, he branded
as highway robbers who deserved to go to Sing Sing.[46]

There was a new relation between capital and labor developing in America, and Dewey thought it demanded of employers, more than ever, to consider and respect "the great claims of a common humanity."[47] Protesting against the haughty attitude of employers toward the workers, he reminded them that "he who stands before you with a coarse garb and sweaty brow, is yet a man," and was to be treated as such.[48] It was not enough to refrain from oppression and insolence; interest in employees must extend beyond getting their services. They were not to be treated as so many horses or oxen; offensive patronage was to be avoided, and they were to be helped to save and to improve themselves.[49] In this matter of labor disputes, with frequent strikes, who was right and who was wrong? Seemingly there was little question in Dewey's mind. Where there was a succession of difficulties, he was of the opinion that the fault lay at the door of the employer.[50]

Theodore Parker, in Boston, saw things pretty much as did Dewey. He, too, protested the way of capitalist and employer in dealing with the workers, as if they were "tools, not as men."[51] The cry of taxation which goes up in our own day was heard in his, too, and he met it forcefully: "To die is their [the poor's] only gain; their only hope. Think of that, you who murmur, because money is 'tight,' because your investment gives you only twenty percent. a year, or because you are taxed for half your property. . . ."[52] Were the employers having such a hard time of it, and did they deserve public sympathy and the legislator's ear? Parker knew what was being said: "I know rich men tell us that capital is at the mercy of labour."[53] But he was not at all impressed: "That may be prophecy, it is not history; not fact. Uneducated labour, brute force without skill, is wholly at the mercy of capital."[54] Who paid the highest rate of rental and the highest prices, proportionately, for food?

Poor laborers! He knew that while the rich, who could buy in quantity, secured flour at $5.00 per barrel, the poor who were compelled to purchase in small amounts paid as much as $11.88 per barrel.[55] Parker recognized and denounced the power in the hands of the employer-class, which could: "manufacture governors, senators, judges, to suit its purposes, as easily as it can make cotton cloth. It pays them money and honors; pays them for doing its work, not another's."[56]

Low wages were "oppression . . . fertile sources of pauperism and crime."[57] Freedom of the press, if we interpret his mind correctly, did not apply to the workers. They "can seldom tell their tale, so their story gets often suppressed in the world's literature, and told only in outbreaks and revolutions."[58] His was a stern indictment of the *economic royalist*:

> He cares not whether he sells cotton or the man who wears it, if he only gets his money. . . . He makes paupers, and leaves others to support them. Tell him not of the misery of the poor, he knows better. . . . He 'makes money;' the world is poorer by his wealth. . . . In politics he wants a government that will insure his dividends. . . . He knows no right, only power; no man but self; no God but his calf of gold.[59]

Could it be that Parker was charged with rearing the ugly head of class prejudice in the democracy? Was he attempting to array class against class? Strange that men, who point out the divisive elements in society should be accused of producing those divisions! But he declined to accept that responsibility: "I am trying to set the strong in favour of the weak."[60] Parker also reminded his critics that "it is as easy to tyrannize by machinery as by armies, and as wicked . . ."[61]

Others there were, too, who made their contribution to the thought of the era in connection with industry and economics. Henry Ward Beecher, not always regarded as the exponent of a "social gospel," lifted a warning voice, where it would be heard, if not heeded, for his Brooklyn congregation always contained some men of influence in the realm of business and manufacture. He did not think merchants, of all people, could afford to undermine "the conscience of the community," for they made their very living by "confidence and credit," and to weaken these was like "taking beams from the very foundations of the merchants' own warehouses."[62] Beecher was glad to note increasing solicitude for "the condition of the laboring classes."[63] Changes were inevitable, if they were not accepted voluntarily and quickly, he was convinced that "explosions and revolutions" would come; and the responsibility would rest, not on outraged underprivileged sufferers, but upon those who held them down with heavy weights.[64]

Were the merchants and manufacturers of the early 1800s the defenders of the *American Way?* While Joseph Allen, of Worcester, thought: "An honest man will be contented with honest gains,"[65] seemingly Horace Bushnell had some doubts as to the number of honest men in business. Whereas in our time, he who would correct evils in the economic system is popularly accused of being addicted with the taint of foreign ideologies, this preacher charged that some men of business were "a little poisoned already by false notions."[66] He thought: "They expect successes just as any specially sharp tool is visibly expecting to cut."[67] It was a low and demoralizing view, which led them to make haste to acquire a fortune. "Trade, in their view, is illicit, and they go to it in fact as a reputable kind of larceny. They expect sharp practice, or to profit by getting unfair advantages."[68]

Channing thought men had other rights than the rights of property. Human rights were superior; men could justifiably claim to be treated as men; but he regretted that: "Property continually tends to become a more vivid idea than right."[69] In the struggle for wealth, individuals became the forgotten men. All should be made to understand, he contended, that somehow "the grand end of society is, to place within the reach of all its members the means of improvement, of elevation, of the true happiness of men."[70] Society, then had a higher function than to erect almshouses, and that purpose was "to save men from being degraded to the blighting influence of the almshouse."[71] It was due a man that he should have more than mere bread to keep him from starving. There were necessary aids to culture and refinement, which could help him "fulfil the destiny of a man".[72] Society was duty-bound to recognize this, and until it did so, it would "continue to groan under its present miseries."[73] Speculation as a means of attaining wealth, and the desire for enormous profits received no encouragement from Channing — people paid dearly for a financial fling of that sort; indeed he was not slow to point out that they were paying for it then. Yet there was something strange about the whole situation. For despite financial ruin, the earth still yielded her fruit; the ocean contained its waters; cities and villages, schools and churches had not disappeared; men's abilities were not lost. So he challenged the nation to move in a better direction.[74]

There were those who thought the consumer was often the victim of bad business practices. Among them was Solomon Aiken, who was the pastor of First Church, Dracutt, Massachusetts, and who delivered a sermon on the occasion of the annual fast, May, 1811. His topic was *The Rise and Progress of the Po[liti]cal Dissensi[ons] in the United [States]*. Speculators bought and sold at the expense of society.[75] Hubbard Winslow, of the Bowdoin St. Congregational Church, Boston, in 1835, watched all who bought and sold, and worked; he delivered a sermon: "Law of Christian Morality as Applied to Mercantile Transactions."[76] Winslow thought business was obligated to protect the interests of all, and came to the conclusion that cutthroat competition was thoroughly bad, that wealth was often monopolistic, and could become dangerous to the public welfare.[77] William Bradford Homer, of Berwick, Maine, reminded men that they lived in an interdependent society, where they needed each other, and that evils, including economic ones, should be brought to view and traced to their origins.[78] Joseph Tuckerman, of Boston, was appalled by the fact that a manufacturer, whom he knew, had fifty applications a day from poor women to make shirts of coarse material, for from six-and-a-fourth to ten cents per day.[79] So he asked for a just wage, descrying the policy of inducing workers to labor for little and taking advantage of their need.[80] N. H. Chamberlain, of Canton, Massachusetts, demanded healthful working conditions and edequate pay.[81] While, by implication, at least, Henry Pearson, of Harvard, Massachusetts, wanted the State to enact workingmen's protective laws.[82] A Society for Employing the Poor, in which the clergy evidently had an important part, was organized for the purpose of providing honorable means of support for those in need. At the end of approximately eighteen months one hundred women had been given employment.[83]

So a number of the New England clergy cognizant of the needs of farmers and laborers, and also recognizing malpractices in the economic system, took upon themselves the responsibility of pleading the cause of the workers and agricultural groups, to make their hearers and readers conscious of their needs, and to throw their influence on the side of the economically dispossessed in society.

CHAPTER IX

THE INTERNATIONAL ARENA — WAR AND PEACE

Religious leaders from 1800 to 1860 lived in an interesting period of history; a time when modern invention was beginning to achieve some mighty miracles. Modes of communication and transportation (telegraph, Atlantic cable, steam railway and steamship) had been sufficiently perfected to reduce the *time-size* of the world to an extent hitherto almost staggering to the imagination. Previously diplomatic relations had all been conducted through British channels. But events near the end of the eighteenth century compelled the new United States to take her place among the powers of the world. Question of freedom of the seas meant wars with England and the North African piratical states. *Manifest destiny* and expansion resulted in conflict with Mexico. Both the Maine and Oregon boundary disputes offered opportunity for arbitration.[1] Here were great public questions to challenge the thought of the keenest minds; here was a chance to demonstrate both militarist and pacifist ideals. How would the New England clergy respond? It is frequently said, "The Church opposes all war in general, and supports every war in particular." We may, with interest, test this contention against the actual pronouncements, attitudes and actions of some of the leading ministers of that era.

There were *pronunciamentos* on war, peace, and international relations almost as rich in variety as those emanating from the period just prior to World War Number Two. What makes this chapter an intriguing one in American history is the fact that both the War of 1812 and that with Mexico (1846-1848) were unpopular in many quarters.[2]

That of 1812 was, in New England, contemptuously desig-
nated as *Mr. Madison's War.* March, 1814, has been described as a critical, if not the most critical month, in the
entire War, when the peace forces, by means of the pulpit,
and other public assemblies, and the press, resisted the
Government.[3] This opposition is alleged to have amounted
to practical treason.[4] Seriousness of the opposition, that is,
among the clergy, may be seen in the titles of some of the
sermons and pamphlets which have come down to us.
Choosing an overwhelming title, Isaac Hilliard wrote:

> *A Description of Christ's Navy, in New-England; a*
> *Description of the Officers and Pilots, And How*
> *They piloted them all into Bull Harbor, and Put*
> *Them under the Command of Admiral Bull; with all*
> *the Hands on Board, and How They all Joined Com-*
> *modore Parrish,[5] In a rebellion against the Laws and*
> *rules given them for their guide, By the Owner of*
> *Every Christian Ship; And how the under officers*
> *in Congress encouraged the people to rebel against*
> *the Laws and Rulers of our Government, By saying*
> *the British has a right to board our vessels at sea*
> *And Take Our Men. And for employing foreigners*
> *and not resigning them when demanded; Showing*
> *that God has forbid us letting of them do it, which*
> *is clearly proved by God's Revealed Word.*

William Plumer, a layman, wrote: *An Address to the Clergy*
of New-England on Their Opposition to the Rulers of the
United States, and Solomon Aiken prepared: *An Address to*
Federal Clergymen.[6]

Hilliard charged that: "We have in this country the
greatest number of false prophets, and in New-England
thousands of priests bear rule by their means . . ."[7] He
maintained that these New England ministers, alone of all
the American clergy, refused to pray for their country in

times of war,[8] and Plumer felt that he was divinely commissioned to remonstrate with the disloyal clerics. They were injuring their own safety by meddling in politics; he held that whenever they were told their faults, "a hue and cry is raised through the land, that 'Religion is in danger.' "[9] Laymen wish, he said, their ministers to refrain "from meddling with degrading contentions, about which they are too ignorant to decide, and with which they have no concern."[10] Plumer went on to say to the clergy:

> You read little in history, still less in civil polity —
> and most of the information you obtain of the proceedings of the government of your country is from some one newspaper, whose columns are devoted to opposition. . . . Railing is not reasoning, and calling hard names is not proof — they are a mean address to the meanest passions of the human heart.[11]

Aiken's pamphlet was designed to meet the arguments against the war and to dispel the antagonism if possible.

Counter-attacks by defenders of the war party indicate that the peace party must have been fairly strong to say the least. As early as 1808, the Rev. Joseph Dana examined the moral and Christian principles involved in the question of war with Great Britain. This pastor was very much opposed to such conflict, in which he believed the Scriptures upheld him. The attack on American soldiers, he said, was an act of individual men, and not of Great Britain itself, which has tried to be quite pacific. [12] On July 23, 1812, Elijah Parish, D. D., against whom Hilliard wrote so vehemently, delivered his *Protest Against the War*. It was a "nefarious declaration of war," it was "nothing more, nor less, than a license given by a Virginia vassal [President Madison] of the French Emperor to the English nation," providing them with legal authority "to destroy the prosperity of New-England."[13] Daniel Dana, too, on Thanksgiving Day,

1812, denounced the war with England and predicted many evils would come of it.[14] Samuel Austin, D. D., at Worcester, defended the peace party; he would observe the day of the Annual Fast, proclaimed by President Madison, but to disagree with the Commander-in--chief; "we are not bound to acquiesce in this war, and cooperate with the administration in prosecuting it merely because it is declared by the government."[15] There was a higher law. Opposition was defensible because it was orderly and did not violate the Constitution, it was defensible because it was in harmony with the tenets of Christian faith.[16]

Apparently Lyman Beecher, like so many in our own day, believed in defensive warfare only. He did not exactly define what he meant by it, but evidently favored enlistment against invasion.[17] However, in evaluating war in retrospect (1812-1814), he was convinced that such changes as were brought about by the conflict, on the whole, were for the worse.[18] "On the evils of War and the probability of the Universal Prevalence of Peace," was the somewhat unwieldy title selected by President Jesse Appleton, of Bowdoin College. This educator-clergyman was opposed to armed conflict, and believed that Christianity sufficiently diffused would, insofar as communities accepted its teachings, uproot the evil. *The Holy League of Paris* (the Holy Alliance) of 1815 led him to believe that war was on the way out. Societies formed for the purpose of creating peace sentiment, as well as for other reforms, won his endorsement, as invaluable aids to the cause of international amity.[19]

Channing, too, spoke out in time of war! It was something always to be deplored, for its fruits ever render it "a tremendous scourge," Yet sometimes events arose to justify it. Perhaps it was "the last and only method of repelling lawless ambition," it might even be "the method which God's providence points out," and under such circumstances "we must not shrink from war; though even in these we should deeply lament the necessity of shedding human blood."[20] In such righteous wars, conscience may approve and the nation deserve "our prayers, our cheerful services, the sacrifice of wealth, and even of life."[21] But he was not running true to form. Time-honored custom demanded that the theoretical war be denounced, and the concrete, specific one be supported. This Channing declined to do. Here was a particular war, which he could not support and he would say so. What could he tell people in the way of encouragement? It was an unjustified war, and there were no valid promises of benefit either to America or to the world.[22] He objected to efforts to destroy the free press. A strange doctrine, he thought, it was which held it to be treason to expose the measures taken by the rulers. It was deplorable that mobs had been incited against men whose only crime was in bearing "testimony against the present war . . ." Channing believed it a deliberate effort to cow people into silence. It was a "calamitous war under which we suffer," and verbal disapproval was the only method remaining to them to obtain "a wiser and better government." He had no sympathy with those who said "that war is declared, and all opposition should therefore be hushed." it was "unworthy of a free country," and if this doctrine were accepted, "rulers have only to declare war, and they are screened at once from scrutiny."[23]

Suppose Channing's advice had been taken! Present and future rulers should be taught "that there is no measure for which they must render so solemn an account to their constituents as for a declaration of war".[24] Such war measures, he held, should be freely and fully discussed. It would, then, be known by all "that no administration can succeed in persuading this people to exhaust their treasure and blood in supporting war unless it is palpably necessary and just."[25] Had his advice been taken, would history have been different?

When Boston was in fear of invasion by the British, Channing felt the city was worth defending; but he did not want his fellow-citizens to fight "like beasts of prey to glut revenge . . ." It must be done to defend rights, and to get an "honorable peace". The victory must be attended by mercy "as well as by valor."[26] But he had his answer for those who felt war was a necessity, however grim. In its present stage, society did not need war any more than it needed "the ordeal, the rack, the inquisition . . ." They were "monuments and ministers of barbarism [which] should be buried in one grave."[27] Destruction of life and property, suffering and sorrow were not the worst characteristics of war by any means. "Under its standard gather violence, malignity, rage, fraud, perfidy, rapacity, and lust."[28] War makes a man cold and hard.[29]

In intervals between the two wars (the war of 1812 and that with Mexico), the peace cause flourished, and not without the aid of the New England clergy. *The Herald of Peace,* a monthly magazine, began publication, in England in 1819, its object being to bring together information regarding the various peace societies and to promote fellowship. Many articles in it were published by the Rev. Noah Worcester of New England. There were also letters by the Rev. Dr. Whelpley of New York. Two hundred seven thousand tracts were published by the London Peace Society from 1816 to 1819. Emporer Alexander expressed pleasure over the establishment in the United States of the Society for the Prevention of War. From December 10, 1817, to February, 1819, the Massachusetts Peace Society distributed 8,298 tracts; 4,785 copies were different numbers of the *Friends of Peace*; 3,513 were smaller tracts. Some copies were sent abroad.[30] In the year 1819, the Massachusetts Society claimed 882 members and the distribution of 16,149 tracts.[31]

Dr. Elijah Parish, the same who was so roundly scored by Hilliard, was optimistic over events, when he talked before the Convention of Congregational clergymen at their 1821 annual meeting, at Boston. He thought the work for peace had begun, and was making progress. Peace societies were being established in Europe and America. What more could one ask? "Mankind are opening their eyes. The sun of righteousness and peace is rising. The black night of war is passing away."[32] This peace movement was still going strong eighteen years later, when the New England Non-Resistance Society held its first annual meeting. The Society had held that human life was inviolable for individuals and for nations.[33]

Henry Ware, Jr., the professor of pulpit eloquence at Harvard, whose father's appointment had so much to do with the Congregational-Unitarian schism,[34] wanted to add his word to the cause of universal peace, of which he like Tennyson in later day[35] dreamed. But dreaming about it, wishing for it, even speaking and writing in its behalf were not enough. He knew that. The question had to be examined, and the evils faced. War was a kind of banditry, it wasted human life, and that wasn't all that conflict dissipated. (A prolific birth-rate could replace fallen men for warlords who liked to play the bloody game.) But what about aged parents, widows, brothers, sisters, and orphans? What about battle-scarred veterans? War burned up, it consumed, it fed on human happiness, and left sorrow and grief for its victims. Moreover, wars fought for high ideals resulted in the destruction of morals. So it was better to lead men away from war toward the ideals of peace, and to achieve the result one must begin early. Parents should engage in this work before their sons grew up to be soldiers; thus Ware opposed giving warlike playthings to boys, lest they too early learn the ways of strife, and not of peace.[36]

As early as 1841, Lemuel Capen, the Unitarian, speaking on "The Education of Woman, with a View to the Progress of Society," before the Barnstable County Teachers' Convention, at Sandwich, Massachusetts, warned that a civil war would come.[37] For some reason or other, a contemporary of his, the Rev. Sylvester Judd, chose on March 13th, 1842, to speak at Augusta, Maine on *A Moral Review of the Revolutionary War*. He thought the colonial fathers were mistaken; they would have achieved their ends without the War, so they employed bad means to secure good ends. Justified they were in resisting British demands, but they were not justified in resistance to the point of war. There was no justification for taking 100,000 colonial lives to secure their ends. To go to war was to embrace the greatest of evils, and no Christian, in his opinion, was permitted to resort to it.[38] Was it a bit of sarcasm, or merely statement of sound fact, to show the folly of war, which led him to point out the patriotism of the fathers in resisting the payment of tax on tea at the rate of three pence per pound, and at the same time to call attention to their acceptance of a tax burden, amounting to hundreds of millions of dollars, for war. He was pretty blunt about the means of financing the war:

> If the government throws into circulation 357,000,000 dollars, without a dollar in specie to back it up, and compels people under penalty of law to receive the bills at part value, and in a short time pronounce it good for nothing, be not corruption and fraud, and the causes of corruption and fraud, then in the name of common sense, and courts of equity, and all criminal jurisprudence, what is corruption and fraud?"[39]

One can almost hear Judd climax his sermon with these words: "No *war* ever was, or ever can be carried on without corruption and fraud."[40]

The War with Mexico afforded another opportunity for the ministers to take their stand, for or against the struggle. Let Orville Dewey and Theodore Parker express themselves. They had their opinions and were willing to share them with others. Dewey thought a strictly defensive war might be condoned as a necessity, but after all there were few such wars. True it was, that war has developed some "powerful energies and heroic virtues."[41] but against these you must balance bad economics: "War subtracts from the amount of productive labor, the strength of all who are engaged in its actual service, and of all who are engaged in providing arms and munitions for it."[42] It is not only uneconomic for the participating generation, but for the oncoming ones as well: "it uses up in advance, the property of future generations; it lays a burthen of taxes upon ages to come."[43] As every dreamer of ideals before and since his day, so Dewey heard men say, "We have always had war, and so long as men are human, we shall continue to have wars." Just as though a love of peace were not as much a part of human nature as a love of combat! As if only Caesar were human, and Jesus were not! Did not both represent human nature? the one on a low level, the other on a high? Where was progress, and hope, and what of the future, if men argued that way? "Do we live in an age when the antiquity of a[n] evil is held to be a good argument for its perpetuity," he asked.[44] Thinking, he said, created wars. To get rid of war, first of all you must change men's thoughts, especially regarding national honor. Dewey believed that: "If those who decree wars, had personally to fight them out, we should have few of them."[45] If the President, his Cabinet and the members of Congress had to meet the

President and Congress of Mexico in hand-to-hand fighting, he was of the opinion that: "We should never have *had* this miserable war!"[46]

Theodore Parker, like the late Senator Norris, of Nebraska, opposed a war, only later to change his mind.[47] But we see no reason for believing him any the less sincere for having altered his opinions. Parker certainly sounded some mighty blasts against the Mexican War. Such conflict was a "disease of human nature,"[48] or the result of it — "cruel and hideous monster," and "What is called patriotism is another form of . . . limited love — a culture of affections without regard to justice."[49] This War with Mexico was "the wickedest of modern wars. . . ."[50] Anyone who held that war and slavery were divinely instituted or approved was depraved and hostile to true Christianity.[51] Of the five evils to overcome, those which men were "to outlearn," war as one.[52] Five months after the opening of the War with Mexico, on June 7, 1846, he dared to say: "War is an utter violation of Christianity,"[53] and as the War progressed he continued to denounce it, so that at a special anti-war meeting in Faneuil Hall, February 4, 1847, Parker openly attacked it in these words: "It is a mean and infamous war we are fighting. It is a great boy fighting a little one, and that little one feeble and sick."[54] Utterly fearless, he went on to say, Mexico was right and the United States was wrong. Not only did our President begin this conflict illegally and unconstitutionally, but Congress lied about it. When some in the crowd threatened Parker's life, he replied: "I shall walk home unarmed and unattended, and not a man of you will hurt one hair of my head."[55] Perhaps his question baffled them! For he asked:

Why, if the people cannot discuss the war they have got to fight and to pay for, who under heaven can? Whose business is it, if it is not yours and mine?

If my country is in the wrong, and I know it, and hold my peace, then I am guilty of treason, moral treason.[56]

Consistent Parker was throughout the struggle. He would have been called an obstructionist in our time. No doubt his influence was great enough to discourage many from co-operating with the government, for he termed it "infamous for a New England man to enlist," it was equally bad "for a New England merchant to loan his dollars, or to let his ships" for the war; and it was wrong for manufacturers to turn out a "cannon, a sword, or a kernel of powder," so long as they were right and Americans were wrong.[57] War, as Parker saw it then, destroyed industry, as well as property; and it wrecked moral values, for in times of conflict did not "the State teach . . . men to lie, to steal, to kill"?[58] Not even the memory of the Revolutionary fathers was sacred in his hands. Returning soldiers were a curse to society — no exceptions were made: "Even the soldiers of the Revolution, who survived the war, were mostly ruined for life — debauched, intemperate, vicious, and vile."[59]

So Parker denied what Governments claim to this day, and have claimed from the beginning of history. Society had a right, in time of need to take his property, to make it into a street; to destroy his house for the sake of the community; perhaps even to take his food supplies in time of famine. Government could make a fair return for these things. They were in a different category than his life and his person. "To these [latter] I have an unalienable Right which no man [or government] has given, which all men can never justly take away. For any injustice, wilfully done to me, the Human Race can render me no equivalent."[60] Did Government have a right to take over a man's life from its own normal pursuits and use that life in armed services, even to the extent of having that body maimed or killed?

Parker defied the accepted code of nations since time immemorial, when he denied it.

How unpopular the War with Mexico was may be seen from the fact that in 1848, three thousand Unitarians and nine thousand Quakers signed petitions asking Congress to end the War. But within the era under discussion, there were those who went far beyond mere denunciation of war. To do away with war, the Rev. C. A. Bartol, speaking on *Individual and Public Reform,* thought the subject of war and peace should be removed from the power of legislatures to decide exclusively, and to be shared by all the people, since it was a matter which affected everybody.[61] Since war and Christianity were at opposite ends of the poles and one must ultimately destroy the other, Andrew Peabody, minister of South Church, Portsmouth, New Hampshire, gave his blessing to the efforts and expenditures of funds, over a period of years, to bring the nations together "under one compact and comprehensive government in a Congress or High Court of Nations."[62] The Rev. Wm. P. Lunt, addressing the *Ancient and Honorable Artillery Company,* Boston, asked for "International law, or the extension of the rules of truth, justice, and fidelity, which are acknowledged to be binding among individuals, to nations in their mutual intercourse . . ."[63] This would be evidence of "the growth of modern times."[64] International law, he knew, was still in its infancy, but as it developed, the world would come nearer and nearer to fulfillment of the dream of universal peace."[65] Sharing with these men in their views was Horace Bushnell. He foresaw a "more glorious unity . . . to be consummated between all the nations of mankind."[66]

It shold be stated that, if the socializers failed to see all the economic, political, religious and racial ramifications, which produce wars today, it was because they lived in a different world than ours. America in their day, was a vast, sparsely populated land, separated from the old world by mighty oceans, to traverse which required weeks and even months — not hours as today. It was a debtor nation, not a creditor, with the bulk of the world's gold buried in its basement. It was primarily an agricultural, not a manufacturing nation. America had a race problem, not in terms of political, economic and intellectual equals, but in terms of a master-slave relationship. The nation was preponderantly Protestant in more than numbers of adherents; there was no Roman hierarchy efficiently organized, such as we know today, with its apostolic delegate in Washington, and a representative of the American president in the Vatican. As compared with the world of the 1940s, it was a simple world. The main thing is: they wanted a warless world, they lifted their voices in its behalf, and subsequent history shows only too clearly that their effort failed; not because their ideals were wrong, but because a wrench was tossed into the machinery.

CHAPTER X

CONCLUSION

The purpose of this brief work, as stated in the beginning (see Preface), was to present some light, if possible on the proclamation of social ideals by some of the ministers in the New England churches from 1800 to 1860. Various authorities were cited, showing that apparently few persons believed the clergy in this era were at all interested in the social question (p. 1). However, closer examination of the works of different scholars led to the conviction that it might be worth our while to re-examine the utterances of the religious leaders of that period, especially when it had become clear that the Rev. Orville Dewey, of New York, had written a two-volume work: *Moral Views of Commerce, Society and Politics,* as early as 1838, and that he saw the social issue forcing its way into the pulpit (p. 10); when we found that Dr. William Furness of Philadelphia was talking about "the great social law of Christianity," and when it became known that Washington Gladden and Charles Loring Brace — names outstanding in the socialization of Christianity — owed so much to Horace Bushnell (pp. 10, 43). Search for additional knowledge became almost imperative when it became necessary to add to the foregoing names those of William Ellery Channing and Theodore Parker, as well as many others, because of their interest in one or more of the so-called social problems. We have seen how Channing thought of Christianity as "a pledge of a social order which none of us sufficiently prize" (p. 8), and how a number of the clergy defended the right of their calling, and were convinced of their duty, to speak out on matters of social significance (pp. 4-8).

In his *Introduction to Sociology,* Professor Bogardus furnishes a long list of topics, of interest to the student of social problems, for investigation,[1] which, although pertinent to the general subject, would have been bewildering to the ministers of pre-Civil War days, when accurate statistics on many vital matters were not even casually collected. Yet most of the items cited by Dr. Bogardus would find their way under the more general chapter headings of this present volume: education, gambling, duelling, drinking, children, women, philanthropy, housing, health, amusements, race, government, the penal system, agriculture, industry and international relations. Summarizing what has been written in the foregoing pages, we note that on none of these larger questions were all the clergy silent, while on a number of them they spoke and wrote freely and at some length.

Not only did these clergymen have a deep appreciation for education, a considerable number of them being Harvard or Yale men, while practically all of them were college graduates; but they gave the subject considerable thought. Bouton and Bacon saw in the educated minister and layman an influence for further extension of learning (p. 12). Parker furnished statistics and asked for universal free education from the primary grades through the university (p. 12). The dangers of ignorance were pointed out (p. 12), public schools were defended (p. 14), methods of teaching were discussed and changes in curricula advocated to make them more adequate and modern (p. 15-19), and ministers served on School Board Committees (p. 14, 17). These religious leaders played a significant part in the founding of educational institutions and in rendering the means of financial support (pp. 18-22). It may be said that from the day when the Rev. John Harvard bequeathed his library and four hundred pounds for the establishment of the university which bears his name, through the days of the Rev. Manasseh Cutler, who had so much to do with writing the famed Northwest Ordinance of 1787, providing for free education for the children of the Northwest Territory, [2] to 1852, when the Rev. Jared Sparks, of the Unitarian household of faith, was president of Harvard, New England ministers have played a prominent part in promoting, founding, and administering the affairs of educational organizations.[3] A glance at *World Almanac* (1943), pp. 543-558, which does not always indicate that the governing official is an ordained clergyman, will reveal that even in our own day of secularism, an unusual number of the clergy still hold college and university presidencies — far in excess of the number of doctors, lawyers and business men in similar positions. Whether this is good or not is beside the point; the main thing is that pastors of churches and other religious leaders have been and are the proven patrons and friends of learning, and by their efforts to universalize the opportunities therefore, they tended to socialize the mind of the Church on the subject of education.

Believing themselves to be the guardians of public morals and decency, the ministers made gambling, duelling and drinking social questions (ch. III). The end of the eighteenth and the beginning of the nineteenth centuries witnessed educational and religious institutions financing themselves by means of lottery, but by the conclusion of the period under discussion, this writer found no evidence whatever of any school or church, with which the New England clergy were connected, that longer supported itself in any such manner. Men like Drs. Henry Bellows and Horace Bushnell took their stand against gambling (p. 26). Bradstreet, of Cleveland, formed his "Moral Society," to combat it (p. 27). Duelling became outmoded, and Lyman Beecher, among others, lifted his powerful voice against it — refusing to be silent no matter how prominent the participators in the practice (p. 28). Pastors and other religious leaders carried on a vigorous crusade against the use of intoxicants for beverage purposes; and Trinitarians ¡and Unitarians were quite able to rise above theological divergences to join hands in the battle against a common enemy — so Beecher the defender of orthodoxy and Channing and Parker, the arch-heretics, alike denounced intemperance (pp. 29-36). The extent to which they carried their war against the liquor traffic may be seen in the number of temperance societies which they founded (p. 35), the ban on drinking which they wrote into the constitutions and by-laws of the churches (p. 36), and the prohibitory and restrictive legislation entered on the civil code (p. 29).

As never before, perhaps, in the long history of mankind, there were religious leaders giving their attention to the question of the status of children and women. Unfortunately the proposed Child Labor Amendment to the Federal Constitution, drafted, we understand, by a communicant of the parish which this writer has the honor to serve at this time, has not yet been ratified by a sufficient number of states to become a part of our fundamental law. But the fault for this failure does not lie in the fact that New England religious leadership of the early 1800s ʰwas totally indifferent to the welfare of the children. Channing, Parker, Bushnell, Tuckerman — all of them great names in the annals of American churchmen — were friends of the children, pleading their cause (pp. 39-41, 43). T. W. Higginson and H. W. Chamberlain, both were cognizant of the evils of child labor and protested against it (p. 38).

Joseph Tuckerman was concerned with the inadequate pay received by women, while Mayo, Channing, Gannett, Dewey, and Parker demanded larger opportunities for women, ranging all the way from limited rights to complete suffrage and the privilege of holding every office and position open to men (pp. 44-50). These efforts, as we well know, did not cease until the nineteenth amendment was written into the National Constitution, becoming effective in 1920[4]. Men like Parker even dared to mention the unmentionable from the pulpit — lift up their voices in behalf of that most luckless of all creatures victim of man's unholy passions — the prostitute (p. 50).

Philanthropy, housing, health and recreation — all were considered to a greater or lesser degree. They challenged the minds of the ministers, who urged their hearers to greater efforts (p. 69), but charity was to be intelligently rendered, so as to treat poverty as a disease to be overcome (pp. 57-60). The name of Tuckerman was destined to be remembered as that of pioneer in scientific social work (p. 58). Better housing, pure water, light, air and sanitation were advocated as the means of improving both public health and morals (pp. 60-69); Channing's views of the situation were eminently sane and constructive (p. 66). If they did not reveal as much interest in public health as we should like, it may have been because of limited knowledge; but even here we find the names of Tuckerman, Dwight, Bellows and Channing associated with the subject — Channing among the first to lash out against patent medicines (pp. 65-69). Recreation, too, while not figuring as prominently in their thought, as we might wish, was recognized. Bushnell, Beecher, Channing and Bellows had something to say in favor of it (pp. 68, 69).

What to do with India, Indo-China, or Burma after the conclusion of World War Number Two, how to treat the American Negro, when the soldiers come marching home? These are questions which baffle and frighten many thoughtful persons. If, in our generation, we have more to say about *race,* than they did in Parker's and Channing's day, it is, perhaps, because we know more about the question, but hardly more about the answer. Yet even a century ago, it was there in the mind of some of the religious leadership of New England; they talked about certain aspects of it, and indeed, they not only talked — they acted. Exploitation of the American Indian was condemned, and missions were established among the various tribes, as well as among peoples of other lands, to offer all the advantages of a Christian civilization to the less fortunate (pp. 71).[5] Protests against Negro slavery were vigorous and effective. Some of the ministers even denied the Sacrament of the Lord's Supper to those who insisted upon the right to have and own slaves and led in the division of churches over the question (p. 80). Immigration, too, came in for some brief consideration, with sympathy for the foreigner and appreciation for his contribution to our American life (p. 82).

Government and penology demanded the attention of some of the ministers. Was the federal system, founded by the founding fathers, to be accepted, never to be questioned? Against the broad outlines we find no criticism. But as ministers saw that system twisted and distorted to suit the desires and designs of scheming men and interests, they did not hesitate to speak their minds (pp. 85-97). Efforts to make democracy work and the struggle for political power in other parts of the world compelled them to think about government (p. 85). Against corruption and partisanship they protested (p. 87). Government was seen to favor business, and some of them said so (p. 94). Not even presidents escaped their careful scrutiny and censure (p. 95). Crime and its punishment were discussed; reforms were advocated (p. 97). Anti-social behavior, resulting in criminal acts, was a kind of disease and should be treated as such, so remedial measures were proposed. While Parker and Channing had much to say, Tuckerman, on his round of mercy, found much to do for those submerged in crime (p. 101).

More people on their own small farms, operated scientifically to produce the best results, and attractive cottages for the families of farmers were advocated by such men as Lyman Beecher, Horace Bushnell and Channing (pp. 106-108), while Henry Pearson tried to awaken the farmer as well as the industrial worker to a sense of his own needs and consciousness as a member of an underprivileged group (p. 105), and Edward Hitchcock made a special study of European agricultural schools (p. 108), with a view to establishing them in America. Parker and Dewey represented those whose clarion voices were lifted to call for righteousness in the industrial and economic order. More modern writers — a number of them — have seen in Calvinism the seeds of the capitalist society. Yet these descendants of the New England Calvinists did not hesitate to point out open sores, such as the Church's own part in upholding the existing system (p. 109), accidents due to greed and speed (p. 110), and the pitiable lot of many of the workers (p. 111). Mass production with its dehumanizing results and the inequalities in the distribution of wealth also came in for their share of criticism (p. 111). There was, however, a notable absence of comment on long working hours, perhaps for the simple reason that these clergymen themselves arose early and retired late, filling their days with many responsibilities; they did not realize the difference between their tasks and those of the laborers. So varied are the minister's duties in the course of a single day that he need never become wearied by the monotony which attends the services of a man working at a machine, where he does the same thing hour after hour, day in and day out, for months, and even years!

When the New England minister did not like his Government's stand on an international issue, whether in peace or in war, he did not hesitate to say so (pp. 119-121), even to the extent of advocating peaceful resistance. To the cause of peace many of them gave themselves heart and soul (p. 123). The State's right to conscript men for military service was denied (p. 128), and international arbitration and co-operation through a world organization were advocated (p. 129).

Of course it is possible to over-emphasize the importance of what these New England ministers said and did in relation to social issues. The very fact that we seek to discover attitudes and actions relating to social problems prior to the generally accepted genesis of the social gospel (about 1885) may lead us to exaggerate the significance of what we do find. However, some seventy-five clergymen, including some illustrious names of the American pulpit, have been quoted in the foregoing pages. What they said and wrote undoubtedly became acceptable sermon material for any number of ministers whose sermons never found their way into print. Yet this writer wishes to make it perfectly clear that he does not claim for the entire body or even for a majority — not even for a considerable minority — of the New England clergy, that they were fully aware of the social problems of their day, that all of them were men of great social vision, or that they had anything like a program for social amelioration. What he does contend is this: here are the germinating seeds of socialization, which were eventually to blossom and to bear some fruit.

While the last and all-inclusive word has not yet been written on this interesting and important subject regarding our knowledge of the social attitudes of the New England clergy before the Civil War, it is to be hoped that the writer has opened the door a little wider, and has made it possible for a little more light to be shed on a hitherto almost unknown era, so far as the social question captivated the mind of the minister.

———— *THE END* ————

FOOT NOTES

Chapter I

[1] Bogardus, E. S., *Introduction to Sociology*, p. 282

[2] Pp., 504, 505

[3] Pp. 146-165

[4] "The Church Discovers the Human Race," *The March of Faith*, pp. 146-165

[5] *Ibid.*, p. 148

[6] *The Rise of the Social Gospel in American Protestantism*, p. 4

[7] *Theodore Parker*, Chapter IX

[8] *The Story of the Benevolent Fraternity of Unitarian Churches*, pp. 4-6

[9] The writer, since his subject deals with the New England clergy, naturally turns to their sermons. There is perhaps another excellent reason for doing so. Apparently the written sermon was more popular in New England than elsewhere, and therefore more of them are available for reference.

[10] P. 331

[11] *Sermons on Living Subjects*, p. 152

[12] *Ibid.*, p. 307

[13] *The Power of Christianity*, etc., p. 16

[14] *Ibid.*, p. 20

[15] *A Discourse Delivered in the Twelfth Congregational Church, Boston*, p. 11

[16] *The Story of the Benevolent Fraternity of Unitarian Churches*, p. 3

139

[17] Stetson, Caleb, "Address to the Society," published with *The Kingdom of Heaven,* of which Wm. Furness was the author, pp. 42, 43

[18] *Religion in Politics,* etc., p. 6

[19] *Ibid.,* p. 7

[20] *An Address to the Members of the Merrimack Humane Society,* p. 13

[21] Ibid., p. 17

[22] Stetson *op. cit.,* pp. 42, 43

[23] *A Lecture on Moral Education,* p. 5

[24] *The Straight Gate,* etc., p. 60

[25] *The Leaven of the Word,* etc., p. 12

[26] *The Christian Man in Politics,* p. 8

[27] *The Pulpit in Its Relation to Politics,* p. 9

[28] *Ibid.*

[29] *The Independence of the Pulpit Is Essential to Its Power,* p. 7

[30] *Ibid.*

[31] *Ibid.,* p. 25

[32] *A Sermon Delivered at the Ordination of the Rev. Ezra Stiles Gannett,* p. 24

[33] *The Works of William E. Channing, D. D.,* p. 159

[34] *Ibid.*

[35] *Ibid.*

[36] *Op. cit.*

[37] *Ibid.,* p. 160

[38] *Ibid.*

[39] *Ibid.,* p. 167

[40] *Ibid.*

[41] *Ibid.,* p. 168

[42] *Ibid.,* p. 169

[43] *Inferences from the Pestilence,* etc., p. 21

[44] *Ibid.,* p. 23

[45] *The New Planet,* pp. 11, 6
[46] P. 8
[47] P. 5
[48] *Ibid.,* pp. 21, 22
[50] *Sermons Delivered on Various Occasions,* p. 195
[51] *Two Sermons Preached at Watertown,* pp. 12-14
[52] Preface of volume II, p. vi
[53] *Ibid.,* II.252
[54] *A Sermon Preached on the Morning of the Annual Fast,* etc., p. 5
[55] *Op. cit.*
[56] *Two Discourses Occasioned by the Approaching Anniversary of the Declaration of Independence,* p. 20

Chapter II

[1] *The American Colonies,* p. 189
[2] Brown, John, *The Pilgrim Fathers of New England,* pp. 91-93, 120-126, 128
[3] Chitwood, O. P., *A History of Colonial America,* p. 552
[4] *Ibid.,* p. 564
[5] P. 40
[6] Dunning, Albert E., *Congregationalists in America,* ch. xix
[7] *Ibid.*
[8] p. 16
[9] *Ibid.*
[10] *Oration before the Phi Beta Kappa Society of Dartmouth College,* etc., pp. 13ff
[11] Commager, *Theodore Parker,* chs. iii, vi, vii
Cobbe, Frances, ed., *The Collected Works of Theodore Parker,* II.46, 36
[13] *Ibid.,* II.45

[14] *Op. cit.*, VII.180-191

[15] *Ibid.*, VIII.31

[16] *Ibid.*, VII.217

[17] *An Address Delivered on the Fourth of July,* 1828, &c., p. 12

[18] P. 8

[19] *Ibid.*, p. 11

[20] The Education of Woman, with a View to the Progress of Society, a manuscript address, p. 12

[21] *Sermons on Various Subjects*, p. 217

[22] *The Sacredness of Personality the Shield of Liberty*, p. 20

[23] *Ibid.*

[24] *Ibid.*

[25] McColgan, D. T., *Joseph Tuckerman*, pp. 140, 141

[26] *The Revival of Education*

[27] *Building Eras in Religion*, p. 77

[28] *Ibid.*

[29] *Ibid.*, p. 82

[30] *Ibid.*

[31] *Sermons*, I.567 Prof. J. T. Fletcher, Dept. of Social Ethics, Episcopal Theological Seminary, Cambridge, Mass., does not think that President Dwight was particularly interested in socializing Christianity.

[32] *The Sources of Public Property*, etc., p. 12

[33] *A Lecture on Moral Education*, etc., p. 3

[34] *Ibid.*, pp. 13, 17

[35] Convers, Francis, *Errors in Education*, p. 7

[36] "Remarks on Education," *The Works of William E. Channing, D. D.*, p. 122

[37] *Lectures on the Elevation of the Labouring Portion of the Community*, pp. 70, 71; and "Remarks on Education," *op. cit.*, p. 118

[38] *Ibid.*, pp. 118, 119

[39] *Ibid.*, p. 118

[40] *Ibid.*, p. 119

[41] *Ibid.*

[42] *Ibid.*

[43] *Ibid.*, p. 120

[44] *Ibid.*, pp. 120ff

[45] McColgan, *op. cit.*, pp. 138, 139

[46] *The Influence of Woman*, p. 5

[47] *Op. cit.*, pp. 19, 20

[48] *An Address Before the Hartford Co. Agricultural Society*, p. 22

[49] *Lectures on the Elevation of the Labouring Portion of the Community*, p. 25

[50] *The World Almanac*, pp. 543-552

[51] Channing, *op. cit.*, p. 25

[52] Dunning, *op. cit.*, p. 300

[53] *Op cit.*

[54] *Fourth Report of the Northwestern Branch of the American Education Society*, p. 25

[55] Riegler, G. A., "Aratus Kent, Minister in Northern Illinois," *Journal of the Presbyterian Historical Society*, December, 1929, XIII.8, p. 375

[56] *Sermons of the Late Edward D. Griffin, D. D.*, p. 53

[57] A few years ago a long-time resident of Green Bay, Wisconsin, loaned this writer a manuscript bearing this information.

[58] *Congregational Year Book*, 1940, p. 43

[59] Dunning, *op cit.*, p. 307

[60] Finney, Charles G., *Memoirs*, pp. 332, 333

61 *Op. cit.*
62 Dunning, *ibid.*, ch. xix on "Education".
63 *Ibid.*
64 *Ibid.*
65 *Ibid.*
66 *Ibid.*
67 *Ibid.*
68 Walker, Williston, "Horace Bushnell," *Encyclopedia Britannica,* IV.873
69 Dunning, *op. cit.*, ch. xix; *World Almanac,* pp. 543-552
70 *Moral Views of Commerce, Society and Politics,* II.219

Chapter III

1 Sweet, W. W., *Revivalism in America,* pp. 2-10
2 Carman, Harry J., *Social and Economic History of the United States,* I.409
3 Storr, F., "Duel," *Encyclopedia Britannica,* VIII.641 "Duelling," *The New Standard Encyclopedia,* IX.486
4 *Ibid.*
5 Carman, *ibid.*, I.411
6 *Ibid.*
7 Earle, Alice Morse: *The Sabbath in Puritan New England,* pp. 270, 271
8 *Ibid.*
9 *The Power of Christianity,* p. 19
10 Paton, J. L., "Gambling," Hastings, James, *Encyclopedia of Religion and Ethics,* VI.164
11 Adams, J. T., *Epic of America,* pp. 221, 222
12 Aratus Kent made part of his journey to Galena, Ill., by river boat; and Jeremiah Porter, the home missionary to Chicago, in a letter of Sept. 17, 1834, to the Secretary of

the American Home Missionary Society, tells of travelling by boat.

13 Riegler, G. A., "Aratus Kent," etc., *Journal of the Presbyterian Historical Society, December,* 1929, XIII.8, p. 375

14 Unpublished letter of J. S. Bradstreet to Absalom Peters, of the American Home Missionary Society Collection, September 1st, 1826; and also unpublished letter of I. G. Likens, February 25, 1835, same collection.

15 Finney, Charles G., *Memoirs,* p. 232

16 Foster, Frank H., *A History of the New England Theology*

17 Sweet, *op. cit.,* ch. VII

18 Sweet, W. W., *The Story of Religions in America,* p. 315. True, Dr. Sweet is citing the case of some Baptist Churches meeting this offense with discipline. But undoubtedly so did some of the New England churches, especially in states where it was now illegal.

19 *The Relation of Public Amusements to Public Morality,* p. 10

20 "Extracts from a Journal," *Sermons by the Late Rev. John Abbot,* pp. xxxv, xxxvi

21 *Sermons Delivered on Various Occasions,* p. 63

22 *Politics Under the Law of God,* p. 21

23 "The Present Age." *The Works of William E. Channing,* p. 171

24 Vol. I, p. 160

25 *Ibid.*

26 *Ibid.*

27 Unpublished Letter of J. S. Bradstreet, Sept. 1, 1826

28 McColgan, *Joseph Tuckerman,* pp. 136-138

29 Gray, Louis H., "Duelling," Hastings, Jas., *Encyclopedia*

of Religion and Ethics, V.114-117

30 *Politics Under the Law of God,* p. 21
31 "The Criminality, Cowardice, and Cure of Duelling," *The American National Preacher,* May, 1838, XII.67-69

32 *The Duty of the Christian to Suppress Duelling,* p. 5

33 "Henry Clay," *Harper's Encyclopedia of United States History,* II.195

34 *The Sin of Duelling,* p. 13

35 *Ibid.,* pp. 43-57

36 *Ibid.,* p. 42

37 *Remedy for Duelling,* p. 12

38 Unsigned article, "Temperance," *Encyclopedia Americana,* XXVI.403-5

39 Calhoun, A. W., *A Social History of the American Family,* II.64

40 Carman, H. J., *op. cit.,* I.411

41 *Ibid.,* II.320

42 "Temperance," *Encyclopedia Americana,* XXVI.403-405

43 Shadwell, A., "Temperance," *Encyclopedia Britannica,* XXVI.579

44 *Ibid.*

45 III.74ff

46 *The Christian Man in Politics,* p. 9

47 *The Works of William Ellery Channing,* p. 99

48 *Ibid.*

49 *Ibid.*

50 *Ibid.*

51 *Ibid.*

52 *Ibid.,* pp. 101-103

53 *Op. cit.,* p. 103

54 *Ibid.,* pp. 105-109

55 *Ibid.,* pp. 110-114

[56] Cobbe, Frances, ed., *The Collected Works of Theodore Parker*, VII.49

[57] *Ibid.*

[58] *Ibid.*, VII.50, 51

[59] *Ibid.*

[60] Worman, J. H., "John Pierpont," *Cyclopedia of Biblical and Ecclesiastical Literature*, VIII.190

[61] Cooke, G. W., *Unitarianism in America*, pp. 350, 351

[62] Bacon, T. D., *Leonard Bacon*, etc., 71, 83

[63] *Ibid.*

[64] *Sermons on Different Subjects, Delivered in England*, pp. 226-234

[65] *Ibid.*, p. 272

[66] *Ibid.*, p. 283

[67] *A Sermon Delivered in the North Presbyterian* [Congregational]*Church in Hartford, May* 20, 1813, p. 15

[68] From newspaper clippings, containing Beecher's sermons, and pasted in a scrap-book on file at New York Public Library, Fifth Av. & 42nd St.

[69] McColgan, *op. cit.*, pp. 177-188

[70] Unpublished collection of letters, American Home Missionary Society, at the Chicago Theological Seminary, March 31, 1837

[71] Hotchkin, J. H., *A History of the Purchase and Settlement of Western New York, and of the Rise, Progress, and Present State of the Presbyterian Church*, &c., p. 263

[72] See "Temperance Societies," Index of Sweet, W. W., *Religion on the American Frontier, The Congregationalists*, vol. III

[73] *Ibid.*, p. 242

[74] *Ibid.*, p. 244

[75] *Ibid.*, p. 199

[76] *Op. cit.*, p. 123

[77] Cobbe, Frances, ed., *op. cit.*, II.26

[78] *The Office and Influence of Evangelical Pastors, A Sermon Preached March* 12, 1829, p. 20

Chapter IV

[1] Mereness, N. D., "Homestead and Exemption Laws," *Encyclopedia Britannica*, XIII.639, 640

[2] Carman, H. J., *Social and Economic History of the United States*, II.50

[3] Chitwood, O. P., *A History of Colonial America*, p. 112

[4] *Ibid.*, p. 411

[5] Commager, H. S., *Theodore Parker*, p. 7

[6] Carman, H. J., *ibid.*, II.49

[7] *Ibid.*, II.51

[8] *Ibid.*

[9] Adams, J. T., *Epic of America*, pp. 156, 157

[10] Griffiths, A. G. F., and Ingram, T. A., "Juvenile Offenders,"*Encyclopedia Britannica*, XV.615

[11] P. 6

[12] *Ibid.*, p. 10

[13] *Ibid.*, pp. 20, 21

[14] P. 17

[15] *Ibid.*, p. 20

[16] See entire pamphlet

[17] "On Doing Good to the Poor," *Christian Disciple*, I.229

[18] Cobbe, Frances, ed., *The Collected Works of Theodore Parker*, VII.40

[19] *Ibid.*, II.46, 36

[20] *Ibid.*, VII.39, 142; V.143

[21] *Sermons on Different Subjects*, &c., pp. 206, 207, 214

[22] *The Works of William E. Channing*, D. D., p. 489

[23] *Ibid.*, p. 447

24 *Op. cit.*
25 *Ibid.,* p. 448
26 *Ibid.*
27 Ibid., p. 458
28 *Op. cit.*
29 *Ibid.,* p. 583
30 *Ibid.,* p. 581
31 *Ibid.,* pp 579-582
32 *Ibid.,* p. 578; 598
33 *Ibid.,* p. 587
34 *Ibid.,* p. 589
35 *Ibid.,* p. 590
36 *Ibid.*
37 *Ibid.*
38 *Ibid.*
39 McColgan, *Joseph Tuckerman,* ch. viii
40 *The Works of William E. Channing, D. D.,* p. 590
41 *Ibid.*
42 *Ibid.,* p. 591
43 Cooke, G. W., *Unitarianism in Amercia,* pp. 331,332
44 *Ibid.*
45 Munger, T. T., *Horace Bushnell,* p. 370
46 *Ibid.,* p. 67
47 Cheney, Mary Bushnell, *Life and Letters of Horace Bushnell,* p. 80
48 Unsigned article, "Charles Loring Brace," *Encyclopedia Britannica,* III.358
49 *Ibid.*
50 *Ibid.*
51 Walker, Williston, *The Congregationalists,* pp. 199-201
52 Cooke, G. W., *ibid.,* p. 30
53 *Ibid.,* p. 191
54 Carman, *op. cit.,* II.79
55 Commager, H. S., *Documents of American History,* I.315

[56] *Prize Essay*, pp. 6-8
[57] *Ibid.*, p. 22
[58] *A Review of the Year*, p. 21
[59] *The Works of William E. Channing, D. D.*, p. 844
[60] *Ibid.*
[61] *Ibid.*
[62] *Ibid.*
[63] Cooke, G. W., *op. cit.*, p. 368
[64] *The Influence of Woman*, p. 5
[65] *The Laws of Human Progress and Modern Reforms*, p. 19
[66] *Ibid.*
[67] P. 17
[68] *An Address Delivered in South Hadley, Massachusetts, July 24, 1839, at the Second Anniversary of the Mount Holyoke Female Seminary*, p. 6
[69] *Ibid.*, p. 11
[70] Mayo, *A Review of the Year*, p. 21
[71] Cheney, *op cit.*, p. 94
[72] *Women's Suffrage; the Reform Against Nature*
[73] *Ibid.*, pp. 15, 16
[74] *Ibid.*, pp. 18, 27
[75] *Ibid.*, p. 31
[76] *Ibid.*, p. 156
[77] Cobbe, Frances, ed., *op. cit.*, III.140
[78] *A Sermon of the Public Function of Woman*, p. 5
[79] *Ibid.*, pp. 6, 7
[80] *Ibid.*, p. 8
[81] *Ibid.*, pp. 8, 9
[82] *Op. cit.*, p. 12
[83] *Ibid.*
[84] *Ibid.*, p. 13
[85] *Ibid.*, p. 6
[86] *Ibid.*, p. 15

87 *Op. cit.*, pp. 16, 17
88 *Ibid.* p. 17
89 McColgan, *op. cit.*, p. 165
90 *Ibid.*
91 *Ibid.*, pp. 95-97
92 Woolston, H. B., *Prostitution in the United State*, p. 20
93 I.2
94 Oct. 1, 1833
95 *The Works of William E. Channing, D. D.*, p. 715
96 *Ibid.*
97 Commager, *Theodore Parker*, p. 176
98 Kirk,*op. cit.*, pp. 213, 214; Cobbe, *op. cit.*, III.199
99 Cobbe, *ibid.*
100 Kirk, *ibid.*, Cobbe, *ibid.*, III.239
101 *Christianity and Sex*, chap. I
102 Commager, *ibid.*, pp. 176-181
103 Unsigned article: "Theodore Dwight Woolsley," *Encyclopedia Britannica*, XXVIII.818
104 Commager, *ibid.*
105 *Ibid.*
106 Dunning, A. E., *Congregationalists in America*, chap. xix
107 "Lucy Stone," *Harper's Encyclopedia of United States History*, VIII.413
108 "Antoinette Blackwell," *ibid.*, II.356
109 Sweet, W. W., *Revivalism in America*, p. 160
110 Commager, *op. cit.*
111 *McDowall's Journal*, I.2, p. 19
112 *Ibid.*
113 Cooke, G. W., *op. cit.*, p. 369
There is some question as to whether this was the first convention; some authorities mention one at Seneca, New York, in 1848.
114 *Ibid.*
115 *Ibid.*

Chapter V

[1] Rowe, H. K., "Charity and Almsgiving (Christian)," Mathews, Shailer, and Smith, G. B., *A Dictionary of Religion and Ethics,* p. 77

[2] *Ibid.*

[3] Cobb, S. H., *The Rise of Religious Liberty in America,* pp. 513-515

[4] Pp. 23, 24

[5] "Respectable Sin," *Sermons for the New Life,* p. 331

[6] *A Discourse on the State of the Country,* p. 25

[7] *A Sermon Delivered Before the Marblehead Charitable Society,* p. 6

[8] *Ibid.,* pp. 12, 13

[9] *Ibid.,* p. 6

[10] P. 5

[11] P. 141

[12] Bacon, T. D., *Leonard Bacon,* pp. 90ff

[13] *The Duties Connected with the Present Commercial Distress,* p. 17

[14] *Restatement of Christian Doctrine, in Twenty-five Sermons,* p. 344

[15] *Ibid.*

[16] Tuckerman, Joseph, *A Sermon Preached on Sunday Evening,* Nov. 2, 1834, containing Channings's charge to the young men who were ordained, p. 48

[17] McColgan, D. T., *Joseph Tuckerman,* p. 162

[18] Tuckerman, *ibid.,* p. 37

[19] *The Story of the Benevolent Fraternity of Unitarian Churches,* pp. 3-5

[20] McColgan, *ibid.,* pp. 154-156

[21] *Ibid.,* pp. 156-159

[22] *Ibid.,* p. 160

[23] *Op. cit.*, p. 171

[24] *A Memorial Discourse on the Occasion of the Fiftieth Anniversary of the Concord Female Charitable Society,* pp. 17, 18

[25] P. 334

[26] *Ibid.*

[27] Everett, S., *Sermons by the Late Abiel Abbott, D. D.,* pp. 154, 155

[28] *Ibid.*

[29] *Lk.* 10.30ff

[30] *The Ministry of Women,* p. 14

[31] *Ibid.*

[32] Ware, Henry, Jr., ed. *Sermons by the Late Rev. John Emery Abbot,* pp. 117, 102

[33] *Ibid.*

[34] *The Christian Disciple,* I.227-229

[35] Cobbe, Frances, ed., *The Collected Works of Theodore Parker,* III.45

[36] "Census," *Harper's Encyclopedia of United States History,* II.75

[37] Riegler, G. A., Jeremiah Porter, p. 36

[38] *Tenement House Reform in New York,* 1834-1900

[39] *Jesus, the Best Teacher of His Religion,* p. 19

[40] *The Works of William E. Channing, D. D.,* p. 587

[41] Cheney, M. B., *Life and Letters of Horace Bushnell,* pp. 312-319

[42] Cobbe, *op. cit.,* VII.4

[43] *Ibid.,* VII.41,42

[44] *Prize Essay,* pp. 14, 15

[45] *The Works of William E. Channing, D. D.,* p. 579

[46] *Ibid.*

[47] *Ibid.,* p. 580

[48] *Ibid.*

[49] *Op. cit.*, p. 587

[50] *Ibid.*, p. 90

[51] *Ibid.*

[52] *Ibid.*, p. 78

[53] *Ibid.*, p. 76

[54] *Ibid.*

[55] *Ibid.*

[56] *Op. cit.*, p. 60

[57] P. 12

[58] Phelan, M., *The New Handbook of All Denominations*

[59] *The Year Book of the Congregational and Christian Churches*, 1940, p. 19

[60] Carman, H. J., *Social and Economic History of the United States*, I.421-434

[61] *Ibid.*

[62] McColgan, *op. cit.*, pp. 435-439

[63] *Ibid.*, p. 418

[64] *Sermons*, I.285-287

[65] Sermon delivered at Plymouth Church, Brooklyn, May 6, 1860; Scrap Book, New York Public Library, Fifth Av. & E. 42nd St.

[66] *The Sacredness of Personality the Shield of Liberty*, p. 18

[67] *Restatement of Christian Doctrine, in Twenty-five Sermons*, p. 341

[68] "Henry Bellows," *New Standard Encyclopedia*, III.162

[69] *The Works of William E. Channing, D. D.*, p. 60

[70] *Ibid.*

[71] *Ibid.*

[72] "Pure Food and Drug Act," *New Standard Encyclopedia*, XX.419

[73] *The Works of William E. Channing, D. D.*, p. 30

[74] *Ibid.*

[75] Cook, G. W., *Unitarianism in America*, pp. 325-329

76 Commager, *Theodore Parker*, p. 249
77 Cooke, *ibid.*
78 McColgan, *ibid.*, p. 97
79 *The Voice of God in the Storm*, p. 12
80 *The Works of William E. Channing, D. D.*, p. 30
81 *Ibid.*, p. 61
82 *Ibid.*, p. 34
83 Pp. 5-10

Chapter VI

1 Nevins, A., and Commager, H. S., *The Pocket History of the United States*, p. 214
2 Bassett, J. S., *A Short History of the United States*, p. 43
3 *Ibid.*, p. 92
4 Adams, J. T., *The Epic of America*, p. 53
5 Bassett, *ibid.*, p. 774
6 Brown, John, *The Pilgrim Fathers of New England*, p. 155
7 Chitwood, O. P., *A History of Colonial America*, p. 546
8 Sweet, W. W., *The Story of Religions in America*, p. 413
9 Jernegan, M. W., *The American Colonies*, 1492-1750, p. 402
10 Sweet, *ibid.*, pp. 414, 415
11 Strong, W. E., *The Story of the American Board*, p. 3
12 *Ibid.*, p. 187
13 *The Voice of God in the Storm*, p. 11
14 P. 13
15 *Ibid.*, p. 15
16 *Ibid.*
17 *Acts and Proceedings of the General Association of Connecticut in the Year 1801*, p. 12
18 Bacon, T. D., *Leonard Bacon*, pp. 3-5

[19] Riegler, G. A., Manuscript biography of Jeremiah Porter, ch. x

[20] *Ibid.*

[21] *Ibid.*

[22] *Ibid.*

[23] *Ibid.*

[24] *Ibid.*

[25] *Ibid.*

[26] Manuscript Report of Cutting Marsh, March 25th, 1835

[27] *Op. cit.*

[28] *Ibid.*

[29] *Ibid.*

[30] Sweet, op cit., p. 424

[31] *Ibid.*, p. 425

[32] Nevins and Commager, *op. cit.*, p. 223

[33] Bacon, *Leonard Bacon*, p. 179

[34] *Ibid.*, ch. vi

[35] Dunning, A. E., *Congregationalists in America,* p. 399

[36] *Ibid.*

[37] Sweet, W. W., *Revivalism in America*, p. 158

[38] Dunning, *ibid.*, p. 399

[39] Nevins and Commager, *ibid.*, p. 225

[40] Abbott,*Henry Ward Beecher*, p. 160

[41] *Ibid.*, p. 152

[42] *Ibid.*, p. 153

[43] *Ibid.*, p. 155

[44] Commager, H. S., *Theodore Parker*, p. 199

[45] *Ibid.*

[46] *Ibid.*

[47] Abbott, *ibid.*, pp. 153, 154; Commager, *ibid.*, p. 199

[48] Commager, *ibid.*

[49] *Ibid.*, pp. 200, 199

[50] *The Works of William E. Channing, D. D.*, p. 689

[51] *Ibid.*

[52] *Op. cit.*, p. 691
[53] *Ibid.*
[54] *Ibid.*
[55] *Op. cit.*, p. 692
[56] *Ibid.*, p. 698
[57] *Ibid.*
[58] *Ibid.*, pp. 693, 705
[59] *Ibid.*, pp. 707-715
[60] *Ibid.*, pp. 723ff
[61] *Ibid.*, p. 725
[62] *Ibid.*
[63] *Ibid.*, p. 726
[64] *Idib.*, p. 727
[65] *Ibid.*
[66] *Ibid.*
[67] *Ibid.*, p. 728
[68] *Ibid.*, p. 729
[69] *Ibid.*, p. 743
[70] *Ibid.*
[71] *Ibid.*

[72] *Significance of the Struggle between Liberty and Slavery in America*, p. 3

[73] *Ibid.*, p. 8
[74] *Ibid.*, pp. 15, 20
[75] *A Discourse Occasioned by the Boston Fugitive Slave Case*, p. 6

[76] *Ibid.*
[77] Commonly mentioned in Oberlin
[78] American Home Missionary Society Collection of Unpublished Letters, dated January 27, 1837

[79] Sweet, *The Story of Religions in America*, p. 426
[8] Verbal statement to the writer by the late pastor-emeritus.

81 Riegler, *op. cit.*, p. 275
82 American Home Missionary Society Collection, Aug 1, 1837
83 Walker, Williston, *The Congregationalists,* pp. 401ff
84 See the various Reports of the Association.
85 Walker, *ibid.,* p. 363
86 *Ibid.,* p. 401; "The Case of the Amistad," "*Harper's Encyclopedia of United State History,* I.151
87 Walker, *ibid.,* p. 402
88 Nevins and Commager, *op cit.*, p. 214
89 *A Discourse, Delivered November 25, 1813, pp.* 11-13
90 See the chapter in this work on the subject of War and Peace
91 *National Hospitality, A Tract for the Times,* p. 47
92 Bogardus, E. S., *Americanization,* p. 267
93 *Ibid.,* p. 268
94 *A Tract for the Times,* p. 47
95 *Ibid.,* p. 48
96 *A Review of the Year,* pp. 15, 21
97 *On Patriotism,* pp. 16, 17, 27
98 McColgan, D. T., *Joseph Tuckerman,* pp. 35, 36
99 *Works of William E. Channing, D. D.,* p. 698
100 Furness, *op. cit.*
101 Frothingham, *op. cit.*

Chapter VII

1 Commager, H. S., *Theodore Parker,* ch. x
2 See Baldwin, Alice M., *The New England Clergy and the American Revolution*
3 *A Discourse Delivered November 25, 1813,* p. 11
4 *Ibid.,* pp. 12, 13
5 *A Reformation of Morals Practicable and Indispensable,* p. 16

[6] *Sermons Delivered on Various Occasions,* p. 40
[7] *Ibid.,* p. 42
[8] *Ibid.,* p. 297
[9] P. 12,
[10] *Ibid.,* p. 15
[11] Bassett, J. S., *A Short History of the United States,* p. 393
[12] Cobbe, Frances, ed., *The Collected Works of Theodore Parker,* IV.91
[13] *Ibid.*
[14] *Ibid.,* III.136
[15] *Religion in Politics,* p. 6
[16] *Ibid.*
[17] *Things Old and New,* pp. 6, 7, 20, 21
[18] *Ibid.*
[19] *Moral Views on Commerce, Society and Politics,* II,260, 267
[20] *Ibid.,* II.275
[21] *On Patriotism, the Condition, Prospects, and Duties of the American People,* p. 16
[22] Archibald, W. S., *Horace Bushnell,* pp. 22, 23
[23] Proctor, E. D., *Life Thoughts Gathered from the Extemporaneous Discourses of Henry Ward Beecher,* pp. 40, 41
[24] *Ibid.,* p. 84
[25] *Ibid.,* p. 118
[26] *Ibid.,* P. 106
[27] *The Works of William E. Channing, D. D.,* p. 630
[28] *Op. cit.*
[29] *Ibid.*
[30] *Ibid.*
[31] *Ibid.,* p. 631
[32] *Ibid.,* pp. 631, 632
[33] *Ibid.*
[34] Bassett, *op. cit.,* p. 287
[35] *Ibid.,* p. 387

36 *The Works of William E. Channing, D. D.*, p. 629
37 *Ibid.*, p. 633
38 "Thomas Jefferson," *Harper's Encyclopedia of United States History*, V.135
39 *The Works of William E. Channing, D. D.*, p. 633
40 *Ibid.*
41 *Ibid.*
42 *Ibid.*
43 *Ibid.*, p. 634
44 *Ibid.*
45 *Ibid.*
46 *Ibid.*, p. 635
47 *Ibid.*
48 *Ibid.*
49 *Ibid.*
50 *Ibid.*
51 *Ibid.*
52 *Ibid.*
53 *Ibid.*, p. 636
54 *Op. cit.*
55 *Ibid.*
56 *Ibid.*
57 *Ibid.*, p. 637
58 *Ibid.*
59 *Ibid.*
60 *Ibid.*, p. 638
61 *Ibid.*
62 *Ibid.*
63 *Ibid.*
64 *Ibid.*, p. 639
65 *Ibid.*, p. 640
66 *Ibid.*
67 *Ibid.*, p. 642
68 *Ibid.*, p. 641

[69] *The Murderer, a Discourse Occasioned by the Trial and Execution of John Webster*, p. 6

[70] *New England Non-Resistance Society Journal*, I.19, I.1

[71] *Ibid.*, I.3

[72] *National Responsibility, and the Duty of Ministers*, p. 27

[73] *The Relation of the Individual to the Republic*, pp. 13-15

[74] Commager, *op. cit.*, chs. viii, ix

[75] *Ibid.*, pp. 170-172

[76] Cobbe, *op. cit.*, III.4-6

[77] Commager, *ibid.*, pp. 172, 173

[78] *Cobbe*, ibid., III.198

[79] *Ibid.*

[80] *Ibid.*

[81] *The Works of William E. Channing, D. D.*, p. 23

[82] *Op. cit.*

[83] *Ibid.*, p. 184

[84] *Ibid.*.

[85] *Ibid.*

[86] *Ibid.*

[87] *Ibid.*

[88] *Ibid.*, p. 185

[89] *Ibid.*

[90] *Ibid.*

[91] *Ibid.*

[92] *Ibid.*, p. 23

[93] *Ibid.*

[94] *Ibid.*, p. 22

[95] McColgan, D. T., *Joseph Tuckerman*, pp. 434-439

[96] *Ibid.*, pp. 95-97

[97] *Ibid.*, p. 167

Chapter VIII

[1] Bassett, J. S., *A Short History of the United States*, p. 345

2 "Agricultural Colleges," *Harper's Encyclopedia of United States History*, I.68

3 "Agricultural Implements," *ibid.*

4 Sweet, W. W., *The Story of Religions in America*, pp. 300ff

5 Dunning, A. E., *Congregationalists in America*, p. 347

6 *The Works of William E. Channing, D. D.*, p. 761

7 *A Discourse Delivered November* 25, 1813, p. 11

8 *Sermons by the Late Rev. Joseph Buckminster*, pp. 301ff

9 *A Discourse Delivered at the Plymouth Church*, pp. 7, 8

10 *A Discourse Delivered in the First Congregational Church, at Harvard*, p. 16

11 *Ibid.*

12 Cheney, Mary B., *Life and Letters of Horace Bushnell*, p. 74

13 *An Address before the Hartford County Agricultural Society*, p. 23

14 *Ibid.*

15 *Ibid.*, pp. 22, 21

16 *An Address Delivered at the Annual Fair of the New Haven Horticultural Society*, pp. 5, 6

17 *The Works of William E. Channing, D. D.*, p. 40

18 *Ibid.*, p. 46

19 *A Sermon Delivered to the Legislature of Connecticut*, p. 7

20 *Ibid.*

21 *Ibid.*

22 *Ibid.*

23 "Edward Hitchcock," *New Standard Encyclopedia*, XV 394

24 "Edward Hitchcock," *Encyclopedia Americana*, XIV.297, 8
    "Massachusetts," *Encyclopedia Britannica*, XVII.857

25 *Social and Economic History of the United States*, I.406

26 Pp. 12, 13
27 Pp. 10, 11
28 *Ibid.*
29 *Ibid.*
30 *Ibid.*
31 *Ibid.*
32 Pp. 12, 13
33 *Ibid.*
34 *Ibid.*, p. 14
35 *Ibid.*
36 *Ibid.*
37 *Moral Views of Commerce, Society and Politics*, II.81
38 *Ibid.*
39 *Ibid.*, I.59
40 *Ibid.*, I.59, 68
41 *Ibid.*, II.84, 85, 102
42 *Ibid.*, II.103
43 *Ibid.*
44 *Ibid.*
45 *The Epic of America*, p. 176
46 Dewey, *ibid.*, II.104, 110
47 *Ibid.*, II.123
48 *Ibid.*
49 *Ibid.*, II.126
50 *Ibid.*, II.131
51 Cobbe, Frances, ed., *The Collected Works of Theodore Parker*, VII.44
52 *Op. cit.*
53 *Ibid.*, VII.42
54 *Ibid.*
55 *Ibid.*, VII.41, 42
56 *Ibid.*, VII.8
57 *Ibid.*, VII.12
58 *Ibid.*, VII.11

[59] *Op. cit.*, VII.27, 28

[60] *Ibid.*, VII.30

[61] *Ibid.*, VII.31

[62] Proctor, Edna B., *Life Thoughts Gathered from the Extemporaneous Discourses of Henry Ward Beecher*, p. 66

[63] *A Discourse Delivered at the Plymouth Church*, p. 21

[64] *Ibid.*

[65] *The Sources of Public Property*, p. 13

[66] *Sermons on Living Subjects*, p. 244

[67] *Ibid.*

[68] *Ibid.*

[69] *The Works of William E. Channing, D. D.*, p. 890

[70] *Ibid.*

[71] *Ibid.*

[72] *Ibid.*

[73] *Ibid.*

[74] *Ibid.*

[75] P. 13

[76] *Christianity Applied to Our Civil and Social Relations*, p. 154

[77] *Ibid.* pp. 154, 159, 167, 169

[78] Park, E. A., ed., *Writings of Rev. William Bradford Homer*, p. 276

[79] *Prize Essay*, etc., pp. 14, 15

[80] McColgan, D. T., *Joseph Tuckerman*, pp. 427, 428

[81] *The Sacredness of Personality the Shield of Liberty*, pp. 18-20

[82] *Op. cit.*

[83] "Society for Employing the Poor," *Christian Disciple*, II.2, pp. 412, 413
"Employment of the Poor," *ibid.*, III.58ff

Chapter IX

[1] Bassett, J. S., *A Short History of the United States*, pp.

465, 464, 295, 313, 437, 438

[2] Adams, J. T., *The Epic of America*, pp. 143, 144
Bassett, *op. cit.*, p. 451

[3] "War of 1812," *Harper's Encyclopedia of United States History*, X.126

[4] *Ibid.*

[5] Elijah Parish was a Unitarian clergyman and advocate of peace.

[6] These three pamphlets are in the New York Public Library, Fifth Av. and 42nd St.

[7] P. 15

[8] *Ibid.*

[9] P. iii

[10] *Ibid.*

[11] *Ibid.*, p. 24

[12] *The Question of War with Great Britain*, p. 13

[13] P. 13

[14] *A Sermon Delivered November 26, 1812*, p. 12

[15] *The Apology of Patriots*, p. 16

[16] *Ibid.*, p. 17

[17] *Sermons Delivered on Various Occasions*, p. 196

[18] *Ibid.*

[19] *Lectures Delivered at Bowdoin College and Occasional Sermons*, pp. 368-380

[20] *The Works of William E. Channing, D. D.*, p. 679

[21] *Ibid.*

[22] *Ibid.*, p. 680

[23] *Ibid.*, p. 682

[24] *Ibid.*, p. 683

[25] *Ibid.*

[26] *Ibid.*, p. 688

[27] *Op. cit.*, p. 667

[28] *Ibid.*, p. 668

29 *Op. cit.*

30 "Religious Intelligence," *Christian Disciple and Theological Review*, 1819, I.162, 163

31 *Christian Disciple*, II.78

32 *A Sermon Delivered Before the Convention of Congregational Ministers in Massachusetts*, &c., p. 19

33 *New England Non-Resistance Society Journal*, I.19, I.21, I.14, I.1

34 Dunning, A. E., *The Congregationalists in America*, p. 286

35 *Locksley Hall*

36 *The Works of Henry Ware, Jr.*, III.122-128

37 A manuscript in the Library of the American Unitarian Association, Boston.

38 P. 6

39 *Ibid.*, p. 21

40 *Ibid.*, p. 22

41 *Moral Views of Commerce, Society, and Politics*, II.237

42 *Ibid.*, II.248

43 *Ibid.*, II.235

44 *Ibid.*, II.252

45 *An Address, Delivered before the American Peace Society*, p. 17

46 *Ibid.*

47 Commager, H. S., *Theodore Parker*, p. 193

48 Cobbe, Frances, ed., *The Collected Works of Theodore Parker*, I.2

49 *Ibid.*, I.37, II.63

50 *Ibid.*, II.73

51 *Ibid.*, III.37

52 *Ibid.*, III.239

53 *Ibid.*, IV.5

54 *Ibid.*, IV.32

55 *Ibid.*, IV.32-37

56 *Op. cit.*, IV.39
57 *Ibid.*
58 *Ibid.*, IV.7-17
59 *Ibid.*
60 *A Sermon of the Dangerous Classes in Society*, p. 21
61 P. 9
62 *The Nature and Influence of War*, p. 6
63 *A Discourse Delivered in the First Church, Boston*, p. 27
64 *Ibid.*
65 *Ibid.*
66 *Society and Religion*, p. 14

Chapter X

1 Pp. 440-448
2 Dunning, A. E., *Congregationalists in America*, p. 419
3 Corbin, W. L., "Jared Sparks," *Encyclopedia Britannica*, XXV.608
4 *World Almanac*, p. 339
5 See Strong, W. E., *The Story of the American Board*

BIBLIOGRAPHY

Books

Abbott, Jacob, *The Straight Gate*, New York, 1855

Abbott, Lyman, *Henry Ward Beecher*, Boston, 1903

Adams, J. T., *The Epic of America*, New York, 1931

Appleton, Jesse, *Lectures Delivered at Bowdoin College*, etc., Brunswick, Me., 1822

Archibald, Walter Seymour, *Horace Bushnell*, Hartford, 1930

Bacon, Theodore D., *Leonard Bacon*, New Haven, 1931   9

Bassett, J. S., *A Short History of the United States*, New York, 1921

Beecher, Lyman, *Sermons Delivered on Various Occasions*, Boston, 1828

Bellows, Henry W., *Restatement of Christian Doctrine*, etc., New York, 1859

Bogardus, E. S., *Americanization*, Los Angeles, 1920

Bogardus, E. S. *Introduction to Sociology*, Los Angeles, 1922

Brown, John, *The Pilgrim Fathers of New England*, London, 1906

Buckminster, J. S., *Sermons by, with a Memoir of His Life*, Boston, 1815

Bushnell, Horace, *Building Eras in Religion*, New York, 1881

Bushnell, Horace, *Sermons on Living Subjects*, New York, 1876

Bushnell, Horace, *Sermons on the New Life*, New York, 1858

Bushnell, Horace, *Woman's Suffrage, the Reform Against Nature*, New York, 1869

Calhoun, A. W., *A Social History of the American Family*, Cleveland, 1917

Carman, H. J., *Social and Economic History of the United States,* Boston, 1934

Channing, William E., D. D., *The Works of,* Boston, 1883

Cheney, Mary Bushnell, *Life and Letters of Horace Bushnell,* New York, 1880

Chitwood, O. P., *A History of Colonial America,* New York, 1931

Cobb, S. H., *The Rise of Religious Liberty in America,* New York, 1902

Cobbe, Frances, ed., *The Collected Works of Theodore Parker,* London, 1914

Commager, H. S., *Documents of American History,* New York, 1934

Commager, H. S., *Theodore Parker,* Boston, 1936

Cooke, G. W., *Unitarianism in America,* Boston, 1902

Dewey, Orville, *Moral Views of Commerce, Society and Politics,* New York, 1838

Dunning, A. E., *The Congregationalists in America,* New York, 1894

Dwight, Timothy, *Sermons, Edinburgh,* 1828

Earle, Alice Morse, *The Sabbath in Puritan New England,* New York, 1891

Everett, S., ed., *Sermons by the Late Rev. Abiel Abbott, D. D.,* Boston, 1831

Finney, Charles G., *Memoirs of,* New York, 1876

Finney, Charles G., *Sermons on Various Subjects,* New York, 1836

Foster, Frank H., *A History of the New England Theology,* Chicago, 1907

Garrison, W. E., *The March of Faith,* New York, 1933

Park, E. A., *Writings of Rev. William Bradford Homer,* Boston, 1849

Garrison, W. E., *The March of Faith,* New York, 1933

Park, E. A., *Writings of Rev. William Bradford Homer,* Boston, 1849

Hopkins, C. H., *The Rise of the Social Gospel in American Protestantism,* New Haven, 1940

Hotchkin, J. H., *A History of the Purchase and Settlement of Western New York,* New York, 1848

Jernegan, M. W., *The American Colonies,* 1492-1750, New York, 1931

Kirk, E. N., *Sermons on Different Subjects,* New York, 1841

McColgan, D. T., *Joseph Tuckerman, Pioneer in American Social Work,* Washington, 1940

Munger, T. T., *Horace Bushnell,* Boston, 1899

Nevins, S., and Commager, H. S., *The Pocket History of the United States,* New York, 1943

Proctor, E. D., *Life Thoughts Gathered from the Extemporaneous Discourses of Henry Ward Beecher,* Edinburgh, 1858

Strong, W. E., *The Story of the American Board,* Boston, 1910

Sweet, W. W., *Revivalism in America,* New York, 1944

Sweet, W. W., *The Story of Religions in America,* New York, 1931

The Year Book of the Congregational Christian Churches, New York, 1940

Walker, Williston, *The Congregationalists,* New York, 1894

Ware, Henry, Jr., ed., *Sermons oby the Late John Emery Abbott,* Boston, 1829

Ware, Henry, Jr., *The Works of,* Boston, 1846

Winslow, Hubbard, *Christianity Applied to Our Civil and Social Relations,* Boston, 1835

Pamphlets

Abbott, Jacob, *A Lecture on Moral Education,* Boston, 1831

Acts and Proceedings of the General Association of Connecticut, 1801

Aiken, Solomon, *An Address to Federal Clergyman,* 1812 (?)

Aiken, Solomon, *The Rise of the Po[liti]cal Dissensi[ons] in
the United [States],* Haverhill, Mass., 1811

Alger, Wm. R., *Inferences from the Pestilence and the Fast,*
Boston, 1849

Allen, Josephy, *The Sources of Public Property,* Worcester,
Mass., 1829

Allen, B. R., *A Sermon Delivered before the Marblehead
Charitable Society,* Salem, Mass., 1860

Anderson, Rufus, D. D., *An Address Delivered in South
Hadley, Massachusetts,* Boston, 1839

Austin, Samuel, D. D., *An Apology of the Patriots,* Worcester, 1812

Austin, Samuel, D. D., *A Sermon,* Worcester, 1811

Bacon, Leonard, *An Address Delivered at the Annual Fair,*
etc., New Haven, 1848

Bacon, Leonard, *Oration before the Phi Beta Kappa Society
of Dartmouth College,* Hanover, N. H., 1845

Bacon, Leonard, *The Duties Connected with the Present
Commercial Distress,* New Haven, 1837

Barrett, Samuel, *A Discourse Delivered in Twelfth Congregational Church, Boston,* Boston, 1851

Barrett, Samuel, *Youths Void of Understanding,* Boston,
1857

Bartol, C. A., *Individual and Public Reform,* Boston, 1846

Bartol, C. A., *The New Planet,* Boston, 1847

Beeher, Henry Ward, *A Discourse Delivered at the Plymouth Church, Brooklyn,* New York, 1848

Beecher, Lyman, *A Reformation of Morals Practicable and Indispensable,* New Haven, 1813

Beecher, Lyman, *A Sermon Delivered in the North Presbyterian Church, Hartford,* Hartford, 1813

Beecher, Lyman, *A Sermon Addressed to the Legislature of Connecticut,* New Haven, 1826

Beecher, Lyman, *Remedy for Duelling,* Boston, 1806

Bellows, Henry W., *The Relation of Public Amusements to Public Morality,* New York, 1857

Boardman, H. W., *The Low Value Set upon Human Life,* Philadelphia, 1853

Bouton, Nathaniel, *A Memorial Discourse,* Concord, N. H., 1862

Bouton, Nathaniel, *The Office and Influence of Evangelical Pastors,* Concord, 1829

Bushnell, Horace, *An Address before the Hartford County Agricultural Society,* Hartford, 1847

Bushnell, Horace, *Politics under the Law of God,* Hartford, 1844

Cabot, Richard C., *Christianity and Sex,* New York, 1937

Chamberlain, N. H., *The Sacredness of Personality the Shield of Liberty,* Boston, 1858

Channing, W. E., *A Sermon Delivered at the Ordination of the Rev. Ezra Stiles Gannett,* Boston, 1824

Channing, W. E., *Lectures on the Elevation of the Labouring Portion of the Community,* Boston 1840

Chapin, E. H., *The Relation of the Individual to the Republic,* Boston, 1844

Convers, Francis, *An Address Delivered on the Fourth of July,* Cambridge, 1828

Convers, Francis, *Errors in Education,* Hingham, 1828

Coolidge, J. I. T., *The Power of Christianity,* Boston, 1848

Dana, Daniel, *An Address to the Members of the Merri-mack Humane Society*, Exeter, 1813

Dana, Daniel, *A Sermon, Preached November*, 26, 1812, Newburyport, 1813

Dana, Joseph, *The Question of War with Great Britain*, Boston, 1808

Davies, J. G., *The Independence of the Pulpit Essential to Its Power*, Concord, 1856

Dewey, Orville, *An Address, Delivered before the American Peace Society*, Boston, 1848

Dewey, Orville, *On Patriotism, the Condition, Prospects, and Duties of the American People*, Boston, 1859

Dewey, Orville, *The Laws of Human Progress and Modern Reforms*, New York, 1857

Dwight, W. T., *The Pulpit, in Its Relations to Politics*, Portland, Me., 1857

Eggleston, N. H., *Religion in Politics*, Madison, Wis., 1856

Eldridge, Joseph, *Reforms and Reformers*, New Haven, 1843

Elliot, Richard R., *Two Sermons Preached at Watertown*, Concord, Mass., 1816

Emmons, Nathaniel, *A Discourse Delivered November 25, 1813*, Newburyport, 1814

Fourth Report of the Northwestern Branch of the American Education Society

Frothingham, Frederick, *Significance of the Struggle between Liberty and Slavery in America*, New York, 1857

Furness, W. H., *A Discourse Occasioned by the Boston Fugitive Slave Code*, Philadelphia, 1851

Furness, W. H., *The Ministry of Women*, Philadelphia, 1842

Furness, W. H., *Two Discourses Occasioned by the Approaching Anniversary of the Declaration of Inde-*

pendence, Philadelphia, 1843

Gannett, E. S., *The Influence of Woman,* Boston, 1857

Gilbert, Elias, *Civil and Religious Liberty,* Ballston Spa, 1810

Hedge, F. H., *The Leaven of the Word,* Boston, 1849

Higginson, T. W., *Things Old and New,* Worcester, 1852

Hilliard, Isaac, *A Description of Christ's Navy, in New-England,* etc., 1814

Judd, Sylvester, *A Moral Review of the Revolutionary War,* Hallowell, Me., 1842

King, Thomas Starr, *The Railroad Jubilee,* Boston, 1851

Kirk, E. N., *The Murderer,* Boston, 1850

Lincoln, Calvin, *A Sermon Preached on the Morning of the Annual Fast,* Fitchburg, Mass., 1834

Little, Robt., *Ignorance, the Parent of Crime,* Washington, 1821

Lord, W. H., *National Hospitality, A Tract for the Times,* Montpelier, 1855

Lunt, Wm. P., *A Discourse . . . before the Ancient and Honorable Artillery Company,* Boston, 1847

May, S. J., *Jesus the Best Teacher of His Religion,* Boston, 1847

May, S. J., *The Revival of Education,* Syracuse, N. Y., 1855

Mayo, A. D., *A Review of the Year,* Cleveland, 1855

Miles, H. A., *Fidelity to Our Political Idea,* Boston, 1843

Niles, M. A. H., *The Sin of Duelling,* Newburyport, 1838

Palmer, Ray, *National Suffering the Result of National Sins,* Boston, 1843

Parish, Elijah, *A Protest Against the War,* Newburyport, 1812

Parish, Elijah, *A Sermon Delivered before the Convention of the Congregational Ministers,* Cambridge, 1821

Parker, Theodore, *A Sermon of the Dangerous Classes,* Boston, 1847

Parker, Theodore, *A Sermon of the Public Function of Woman,* Boston, 1853

Patton, W. W., *Duty of Christians to Suppress Duelling,* Boston, 1844

Peabody, Andrew, *The Nature and Influence of War,* Boston, 1843

Pearson, Henry B., *A Discourse Delivered in the First Congregational Church, at Harvard, Mass.,* Boston, 1848

Phelan, M., *The New Handbook of All Denominations,* Nashville, 1930

Plumer, William, *An Address to the Clergy of New-England,* etc., Concord, 1814

Stetson, Caleb, *A Discourse on the State of the Country,* Boston, 1842

Stow, Timothy, *National Responsibility and the Duty of Ministers,* Rochester, 1846

Thayer, T. B., *The Christian Man in Politics,* Boston, 1860

Tuckerman, Joseph, *A Sermon Preached on Sunday Evening, November 2,* 1834, Boston, 1834

Tuckerman, Joseph, *Prize Essay,* Philadelphia, 1830

Veiller, Lawrence, *Tenement House Reform,* New York, 1900

Wilson, Joseph G., *The Voice of God in the Storm,* Lafayette, 184

Woods, Leonard, D. D., *Duties of the Rich,* Andover, 1827

Periodicals

The Christian Disciple and Theological Review, Boston, 1819-1821

The American National Preacher, New York

McDowall's Journal, New York, 1834

New England Non-Resistance Society Journal, Boston, 1840

Unpublished Materials

American Board of Commissioners for Foreign Missions
Letters and Reports

American Home Missionary Society Letters and Reports

INDEX

179